first phrases
FRENCH

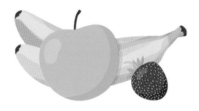

ACKNOWLEDGMENTS

Publishing Director	Piers Pickard
Publisher	Hanna Otero
Commissioning Editor	Catharine Robertson
Project Management	Duck Egg Blue
Illustrators	Andy Mansfield
	Kait Eaton
	Sebastian Iwohn
Design	Duck Egg Blue
Print Production	Lisa Taylor

With thanks to Emma Burton, Jean-Pierre Masclef, Cheree Broughton, and Jennifer Dixon

Published in June 2020 by Lonely Planet Global Ltd
CRN: 554153
ISBN: 978 1 83869 093 9
www.lonelyplanet.com/kids
© Lonely Planet 2020
Printed in China

10 9 8 7 6 5 4 3 2

Lonely Planet Office

IRELAND
Digital Depot, Roe Lane (off Thomas St), Digital Hub, Dublin 8, D08 TCV4

STAY IN TOUCH lonelyplanet.com/contact

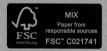

lonely planet
Kids

first phrases
FRENCH

Quel métier
aimerais-tu?

Je veux
être artiste.

Illustrated by
Andy Mansfield, Kait Eaton & Sebastian Iwohn

Contents

How to use this book

Hello and bonjour! This book is full of useful French phrases to help you start speaking the language. The speech balloon below shows how each phrase is displayed in the book. At the top is the phrase in English. Below that is the phrase in French. And below that is the pronunciation to help you sound out the French words. Try reading the phrases in the book aloud. Practice them with friends, family, and whenever you can!

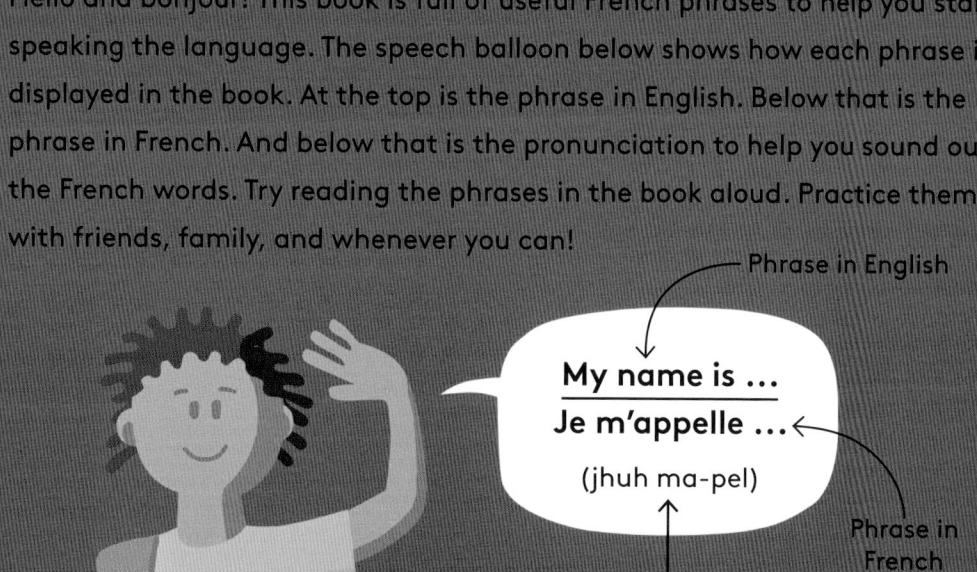

Phrase in English

My name is …
Je m'appelle …

(jhuh ma-pel)

Phrase in French

Pronunciation

Pronunciation notes

Words are made up of syllables, which could be described as individual sounds, or beats. A hyphen in the pronunciation shows where one syllable ends and the next begins.

The single vowel sounds in the pronunciation have been written phonetically, meaning they should be pronounced in the following way:

A as in "apple"   E as in "egg"
I as in "igloo"   O as in "orange"
U as in "umbrella"

Y is pronounced as it sounds in "yellow"

About the language

The French language has its own set of rules. Here are some grammar guidelines to keep in mind. This book will give you additional helpful notes as you go along, too.

Nouns

A noun is a word that refers to a person, place, or thing. Every noun in French is either masculine (m) or feminine (f). This is its gender, and it affects many of the words around the noun.

TIP!
Always try to learn French nouns with le, la, un, or une so that you remember their gender.

Le, la, or les

For "**the**," you say "**le**" (pronounced "luh") or "**la**" (la) depending on the gender of the noun. If a noun is masculine, you say **le**. If a noun is feminine, you say **la**. If the noun starts with a vowel, you use an apostrophe: **l'**.

the boy	the girl	the tree
le garçon	la fille	l'arbre
(luh gar-son)	(la fee)	(lar-bruh)

If the noun is plural (meaning there is more than one of them), you say "**les**" (lay). If the noun starts with a vowel, you pronounce the "**s**" (layz).

the boys	the girls	the trees
les garçons	les filles	les arbres
(lay gar-son)	(lay fee)	(layz ar-bruh)

Un or une

For "a," you say "un" (uh) or "une" (oon). If a noun is masculine, you say un.
If a noun is feminine, you say une.

a dog	a house
un chien	une maison
(uh shee-eh)	(oon may-zon)

Plurals

To make most nouns plurals, you add -s at the end. This isn't usually
pronounced. For nouns ending in -au and -eau, you add an x instead of s.

the cats	the boats
les chats	les bateaux
(lay sha)	(lay ba-toh)

Adjectives

Adjectives are words that describe a noun. In French, they change depending
on whether the noun is masculine, feminine, or plural. If the noun is feminine,
you usually add -e at the end. If the noun is plural, you usually add -s if it's
masculine and -es if it's feminine.

He is small	She is small	They are small	The girls are small
Il est petit	Elle est petite	Ils sont petits	Les filles sont petites
(eel eh ptee)	(el eh pteet)	(eel son ptee)	(lay fee son pteet)

Pronouns

Pronouns (such as "**he**," "**she**," "**yours**") replace a noun. For example, instead of saying "The boy is eating," you could say "He is eating." The one you use depends on whether the noun is masculine, feminine, or plural.

Pronoun	Translation	Pronunciation
I	**je**	(jhuh)
you (singular or informal)	**tu**	(too)
he/it (m)	**il**	(eel)
she/it (f)	**elle**	(el)
we	**nous**	(noo)
you (plural or formal)	**vous**	(voo)
they (m)	**ils**	(eel)
they (f)	**elles**	(el)

Tu or vous

"**You**" can be either "**tu**" (too) or "**vous**" (voo). You use **tu** for friends and close family, and **vous** when you want to be more formal, like when you're talking to teachers or grown-ups you don't know very well. If there is more than one person, you always use **vous**.

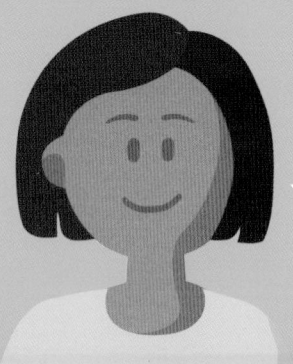

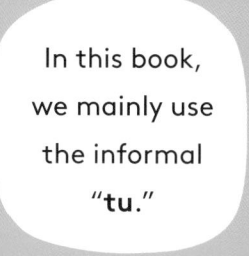

In this book, we mainly use the informal "**tu**."

9

Ils or elles

For "**they**," you say "**ils**" (eel) or "**elles**" (el). For more than one masculine object or person, you say **ils**. For more than one feminine object or person, you say **elles**. If there are both masculine and feminine nouns in the group, you say **ils**.

the boys	the girls	the boys and girls
ils	elles	ils
(eel)	(el)	(eel)

My and your

For "**my**," you say "**mon**" (mon) if the noun is masculine and "**ma**" (ma) if the noun is feminine. For "**your**," you say "**ton**" (ton) if the noun is masculine and "**ta**" (ta) if the noun is feminine. If the noun is plural, you say "**mes**" (may) for "**my**" and "**tes**" (tay) for "**your**." If you are speaking to someone more formally, such as a teacher or a grown-up you don't know very well, for "**your**" you say "**vos**" (voh).

Singular nouns

my bag	my key	your flower	your brother
mon sac	ma clé	ta fleur	ton frère
(mon sak)	(ma klay)	(ta fluhr)	(ton frair)

Plural nouns

my parents	my friends	your cookies	your books
mes parents	mes amis	tes biscuits	vos livres
(may pa-ron)	(mayz am-ee)	(tay bee-skwee)	(voh leev-ruh)

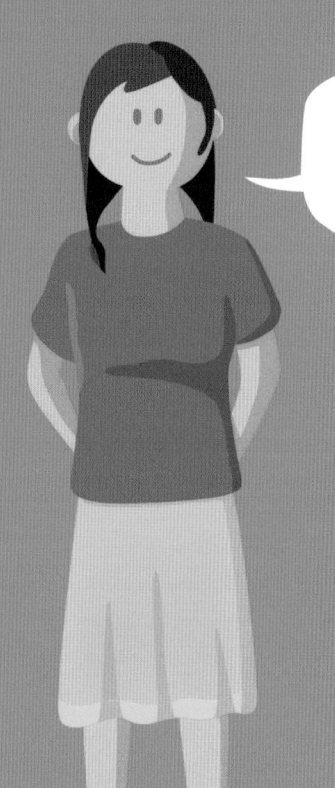

Are you ready?
Es-tu prêt?
(eh-too preh)

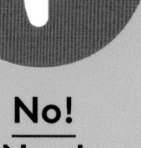

Yes!
Oui!
(wee)

No!
Non!
(non)

Maybe
Peut-être
(puh-tair-tr)

Hi!
Salut!
(sa-loo)

Hello
Bonjour
(bon-jhoor)

"Salut" can mean "hello," "hi," or even "bye"!

sun
le soleil
(luh soh-lay)
↓

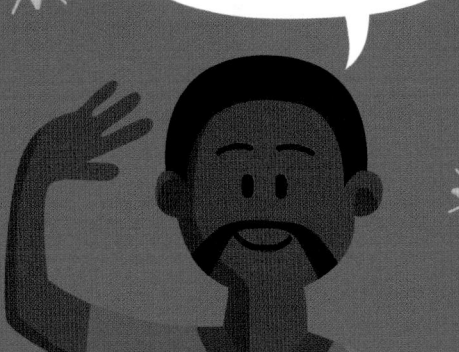

Good night
Bonne nuit
(bon nwee)

See you later
À tout à l'heure
(a toot a luhr)

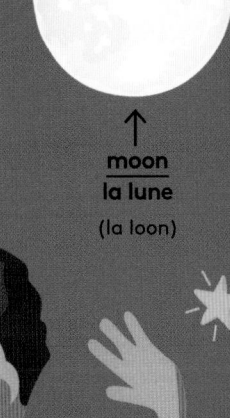

↑
moon
la lune
(la loon)

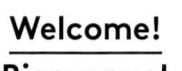
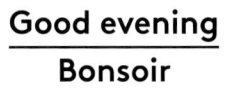
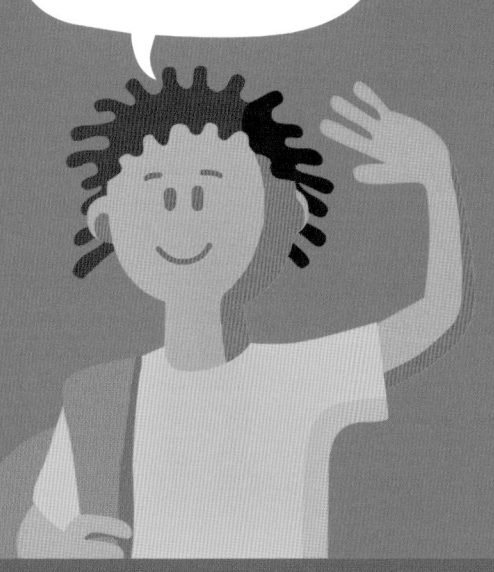
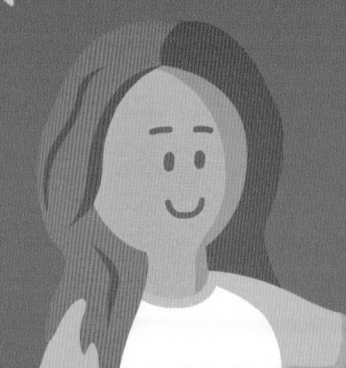
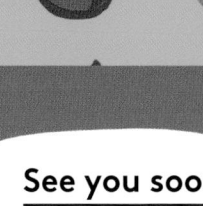
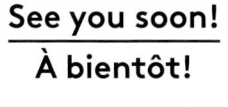
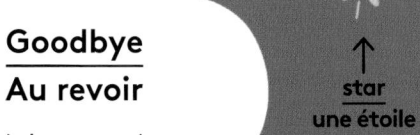
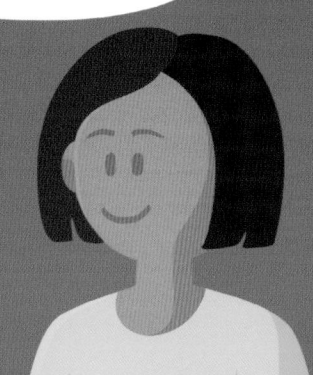

How are you?
Comment allez-vous?

(ko-mont a-lay-voo)

If you are greeting a friend, say "Comment vas-tu?" Or you could say "Comment ça va?" or simply "Ça va?"

I'm ...
Ça va ...

(sa va)

very well
très bien

(tray bee-an)

OK
comme çi comme ça

(kom see kom sa)

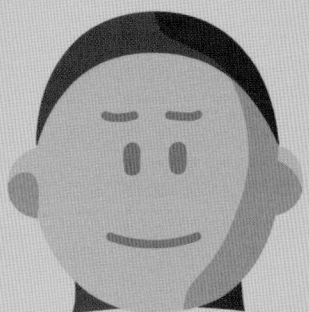

not good
mal

(mal)

Please
S'il vous plaît

(seel voo pleh)

Thank you
Merci

(mair-see)

Thank you very much
Merci beaucoup

(mair-see boh-koo)

You're welcome
Je vous en prie

(jhuh vooz-on pree)

It's nothing
De rien

(duh ree-an)

With pleasure
Avec plaisir

(a-vek play-zeer)

Sorry
Pardon

(par-don)

Excuse me
Excusez-moi

(ek-skew-zay-mwah)

15

See pages 154–155 for a list of country names.

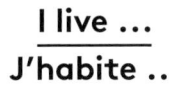

I live …
<u>J'habite …</u>

(jha-beet)

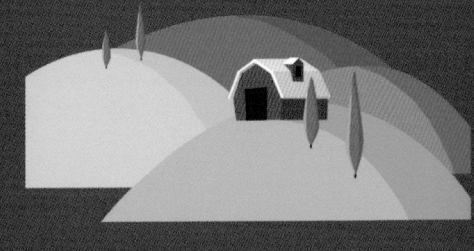

<u>in the countryside</u>
à la campagne

(a la kom-pan-yuh)

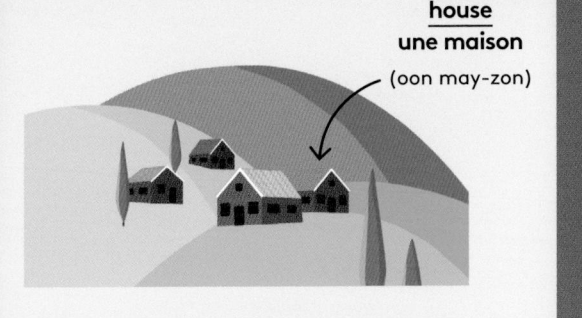

house
une maison
(oon may-zon)

<u>in a village</u>
dans un village

(donz uh vee-la-jh)

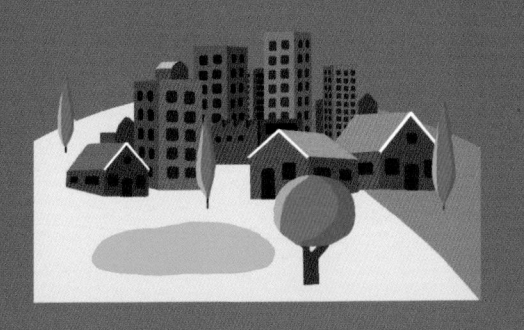

<u>in a town</u>
dans une ville

(donz oon veel)

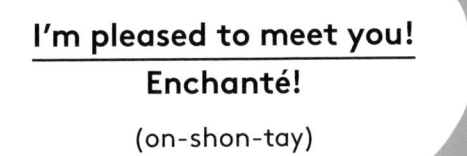

<u>in a city</u>
dans une grande ville

(donz oon grond veel)

<u>I'm pleased to meet you!</u>
Enchanté!

(on-shon-tay)

17

To say how old you are, you say how many years you have.

"J'ai" means "I have," so if you are ten you say "J'ai dix ans." This means "I have ten years."

How old are you?
Quel âge as-tu?

(kel ar-jh a-too)

I'm ... years old.
J'ai ... ans.

(jhay ... on)

1
one
un
(uh)

2
two
deux
(duh)

7
seven
sept
(set)

8
eight
huit
(hweet)

13
thirteen
treize
(trehz)

14
fourteen
quatorze
(ka-torz)

15
fifteen
quinze
(kanz)

16
sixteen
seize
(sehz)

30
thirty
trente
(trahnt)

40
forty
quarante
(ka-rahnt)

50
fifty
cinquante
(san-kahnt)

60
sixty
soixante
(swa-sahnt)

3 three trois (twah)	**4** four quatre (kat-r)	**5** five cinq (sank)	**6** six six (sees)
9 nine neuf (nuhf)	**10** ten dix (dees)	**11** eleven onze (onz)	**12** twelve douze (dooz)
17 seventeen dix-sept (dees-set)	**18** eighteen dix-huit (dees-hweet)	**19** nineteen dix-neuf (dees-nuhf)	**20** twenty vingt (vahn)
70 seventy soixante-dix (swa-sahnt-dees)	**80** eighty quatre-vingts (kat-r-vahn)	**90** ninety quatre-vingt-dix (kat-r-vahn-dees)	**100** one hundred cent (sahnt)

When is your birthday?
C'est quand ton anniversaire?

(seh kahn ton an-ee-vair-sair)

My birthday is …
Mon anniversaire c'est …

(mon an-ee-vair-sair seh)

today
aujourd'hui

(oh-jhoor-dwee)

tomorrow
demain

(duh-ma)

next week
la semaine prochaine

(la suh-men pro-shen)

on Sunday
dimanche

(dee-monsh)

on Monday
lundi

(lun-dee)

on Tuesday
mardi

(mar-dee)

on Wednesday
mercredi

(meh-kreh-dee)

on Thursday
jeudi

(jhuh-dee)

on Friday
vendredi

(von-dre-dee)

on Saturday
samedi

(sam-dee)

20

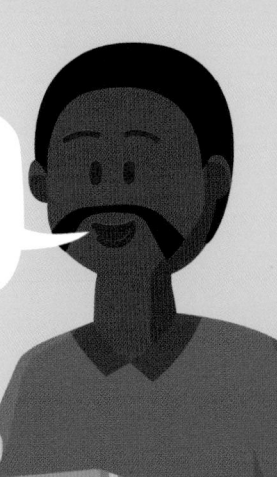
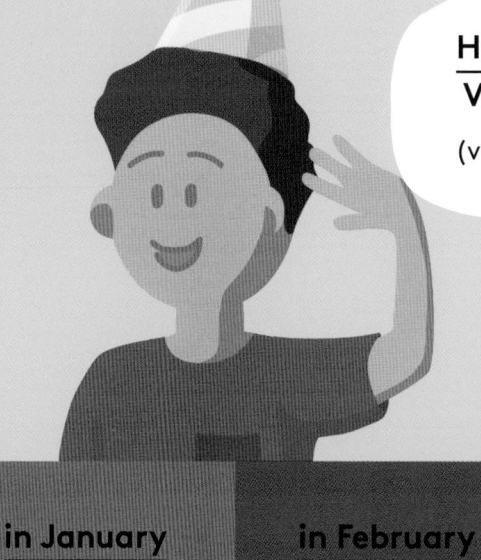

Happy birthday!
Bon anniversaire!

(bon an-ee-vair-sair)

Here is a present.
Voici un cadeau.

(vwa-see uh ca-doh)

In French, days of the week and months don't start with a capital letter.

in January
en janvier

(on jhan-vee-ay)

in February
en février

(on fay-vree-ay)

in March
en mars

(on marz)

in April
en avril

(on a-vreel)

in May
en mai

(on may)

in June
en juin

(on jhoo-ahn)

in July
en juillet

(on jhwee-ay)

in August
en août

(on oot)

in September
en septembre

(on sep-tom-bruh)

in October
en octobre

(on ok-toh-bruh)

in November
en novembre

(on noh-vom-bruh)

in December
en décembre

(on day-som-bruh)

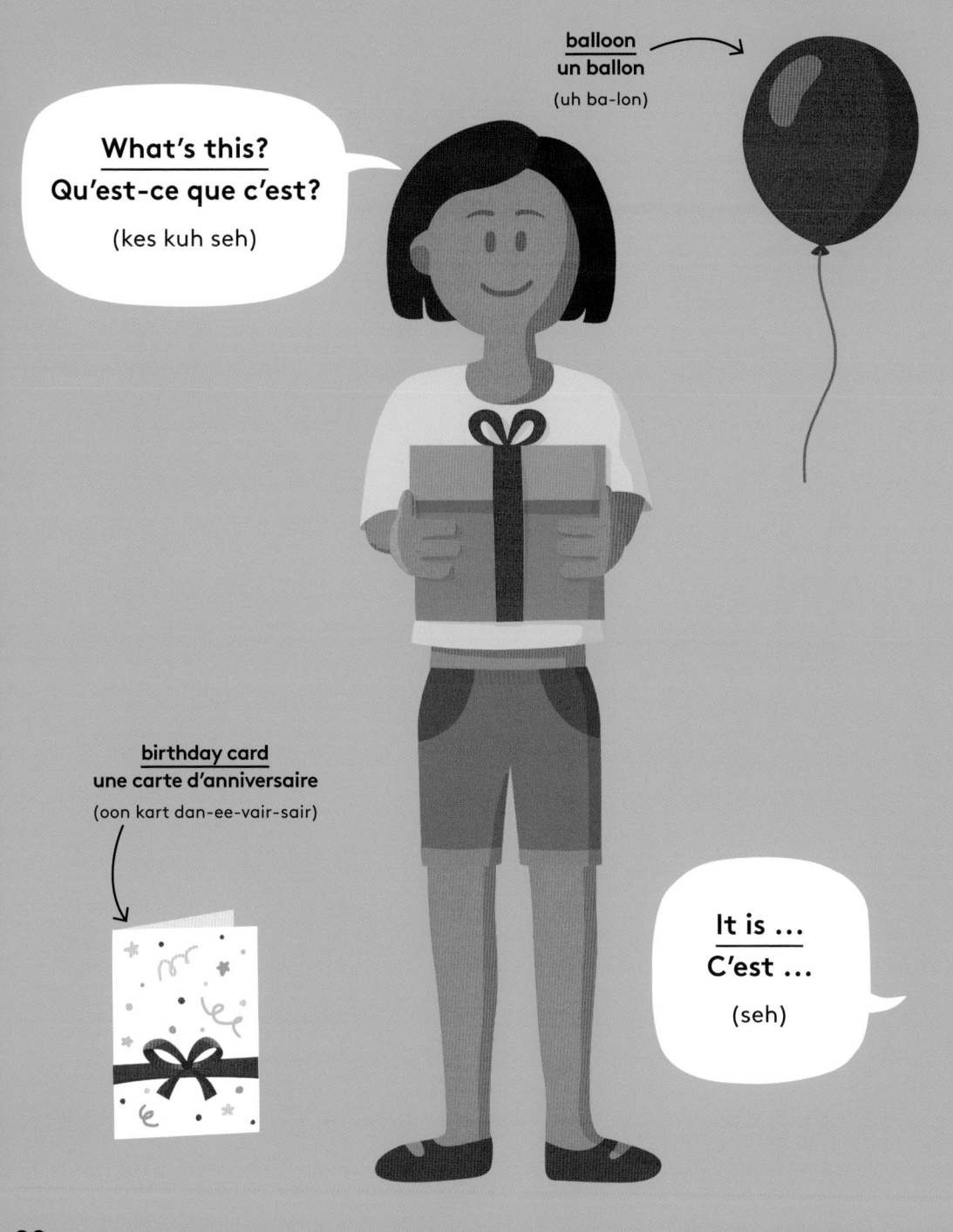

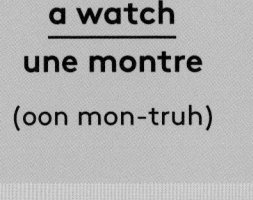

a watch
une montre

(oon mon-truh)

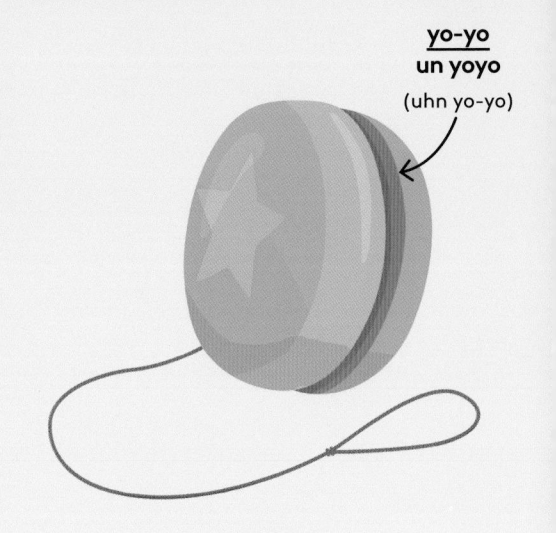

yo-yo
un yoyo

(uhn yo-yo)

a toy
un jouet

(uh jhoo-ay)

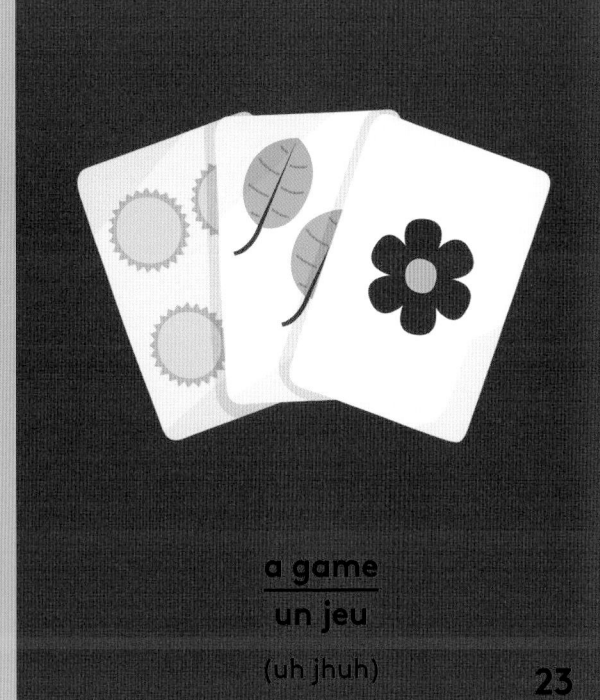

a necklace
un collier

(uh coh-lee-eh)

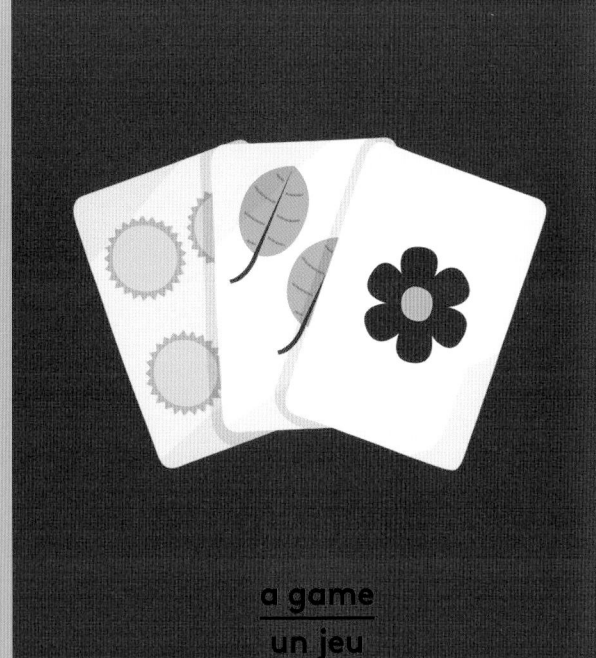

a game
un jeu

(uh jhuh)

23

What color is it?
C'est de quelle couleur?
(seh duh kel koo-lur)

It is …
C'est …
(seh)

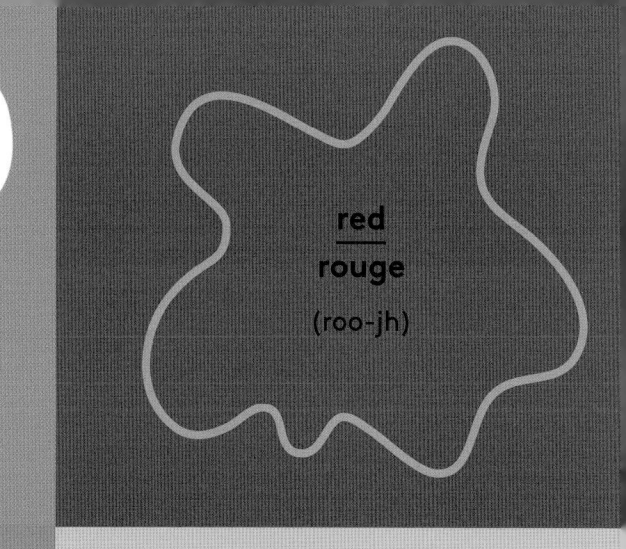

red
rouge
(roo-jh)

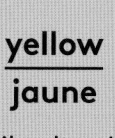

blue
bleu
(bluh)

yellow
jaune
(jh-ohwn)

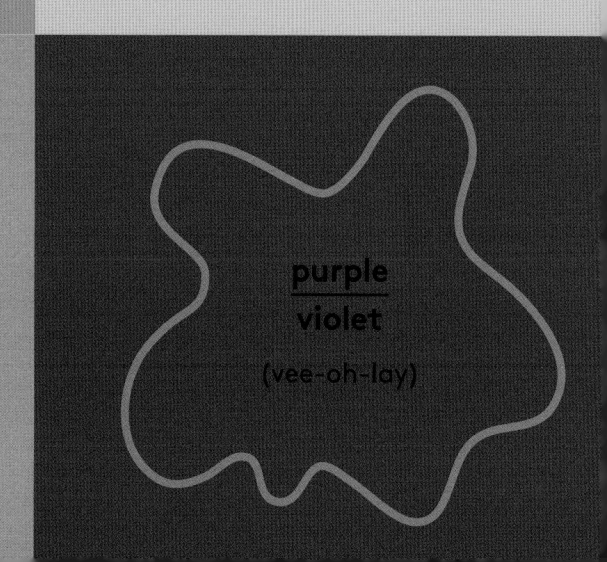

orange
orange
(o-ran-jh)

purple
violet
(vee-oh-lay)

24

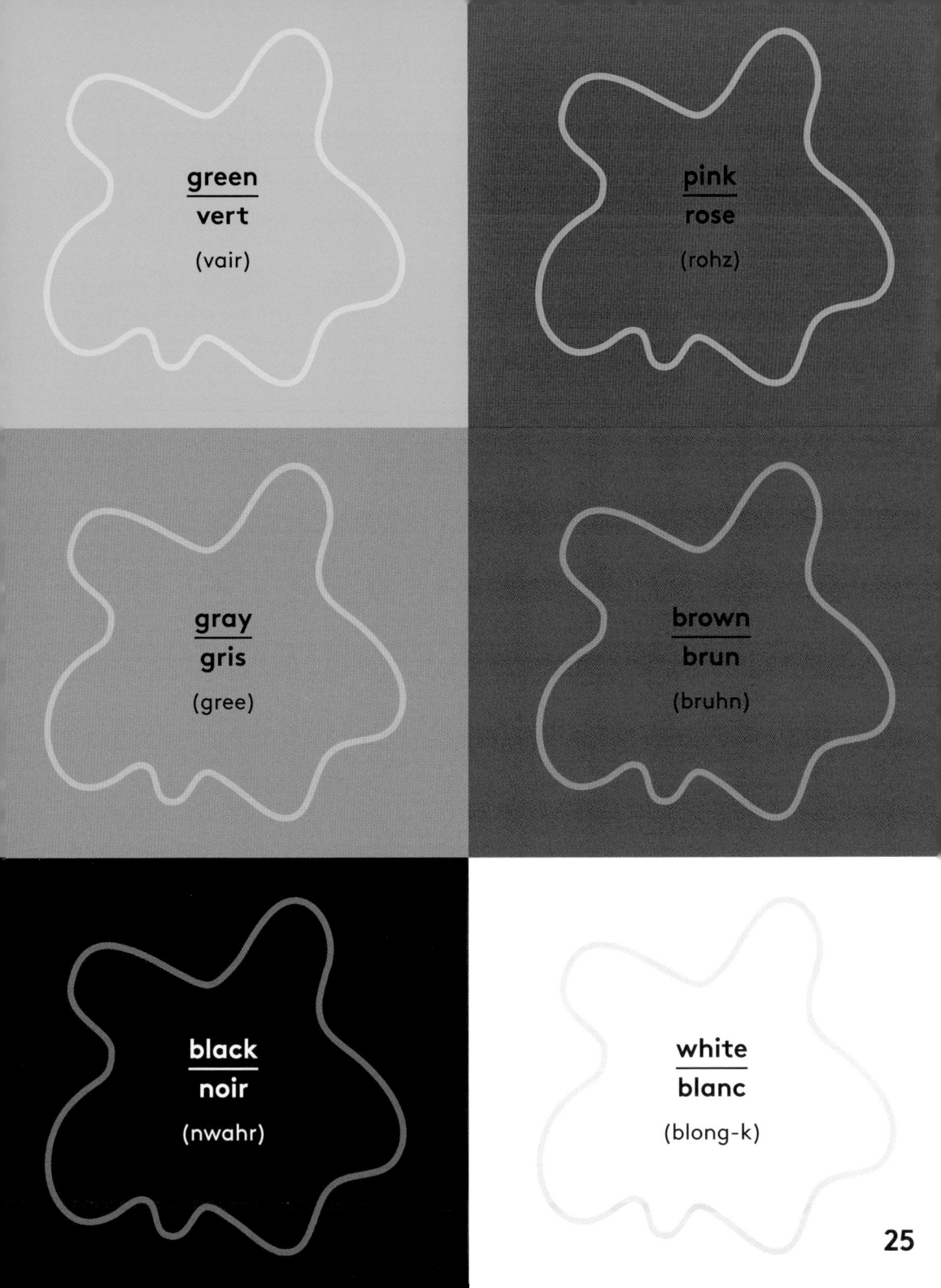

green

vert

(vair)

pink

rose

(rohz)

gray

gris

(gree)

brown

brun

(bruhn)

black

noir

(nwahr)

white

blanc

(blong-k)

25

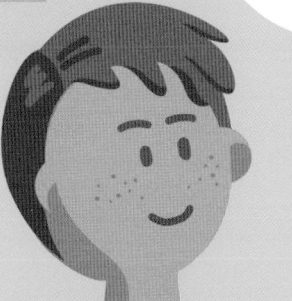

Just like days and months, languages don't begin with a capital letter in French. Countries do though!

What languages do you speak?
Quelles langues parles-tu?
(kel long parl-too)

I speak ...
Je parle ...
(jhuh parl)

French
français
(fron-say)

English
anglais
(ong-lay)

Chinese
chinois
(shin-wah)

Russian
russe
(rooss)

Spanish
espagnol
(es-pan-yol)

German
allemand
(al-mon)

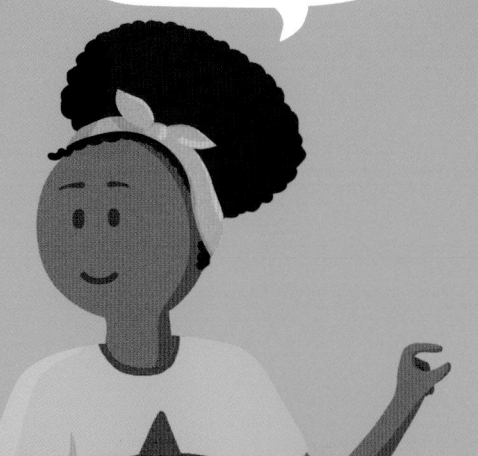

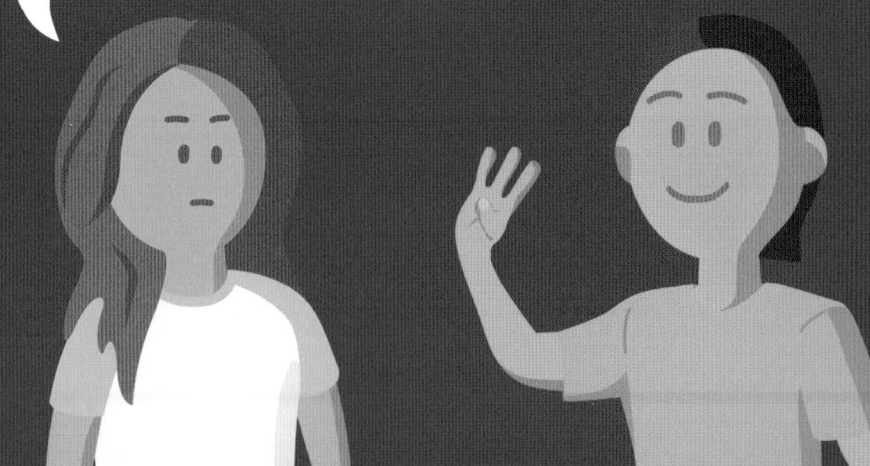

I'm sorry. I don't understand.
Je suis désolé. Je ne comprends pas.

(jhuh swee dez-oh-lay jhuh nuh com-prond pa)

Could you speak more slowly?
Pourrais-tu parler plus lentement?

(poo-ray-too par-lay ploo lon-tuhr-moh)

What does this say?
Qu'est-ce que ça veut dire?

(kes kuh sa vuh deer)

It says "Keep off the grass."
Ça dit "Pelouse interdite."

(sa dee pel-ooz an-tair-dee)

sign
un panneau
(uh pan-oh)

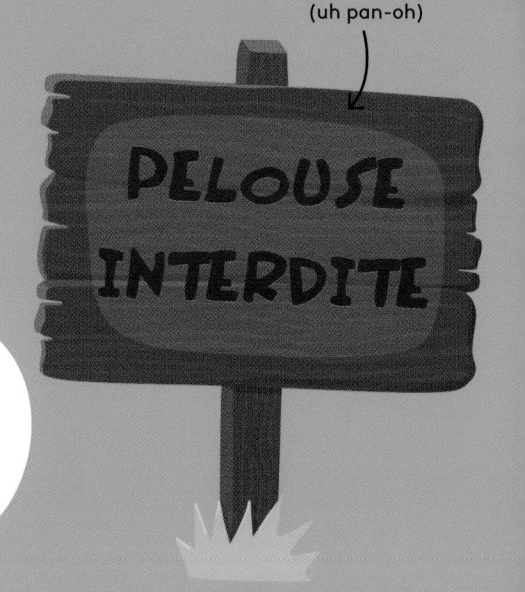

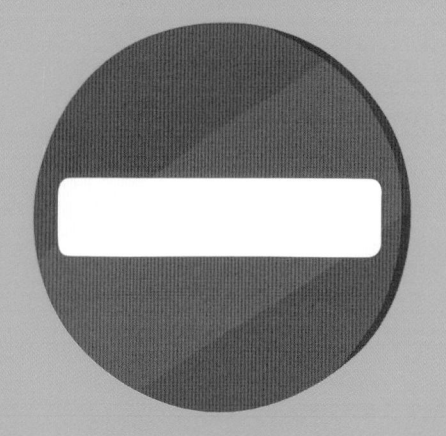

No entry!
Sens interdit!

(sons an-tair-dee)

Warning!
Attention!

(a-ton-see-on)

Do not touch!
Ne touchez pas!

(nuh too-shay pa)

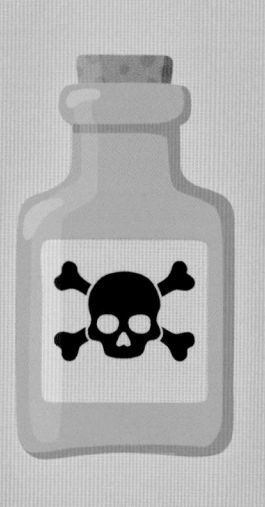

Poison!
Le poison!

(luh pwa-zon)

Help!
Au secours!
(oh s-koor)

It's an emergency!
C'est un cas d'urgence!
(seh uh kas duhr-jhons)

Watch out!
Faites attention!
(feht a-ton-see-on)

Stop!
Arrêtez!
(a-reh-tay)

I need the police!
J'ai besoin de la police!
(jhay buh-zwan duh la po-lees)

There's a fire!
Il y a un feu!
(eel ya uh fuh)

Please call an ambulance.
Appelez une ambulance s'il vous plaît.
(ap-lay oon am-boo-lons seel voo pleh)

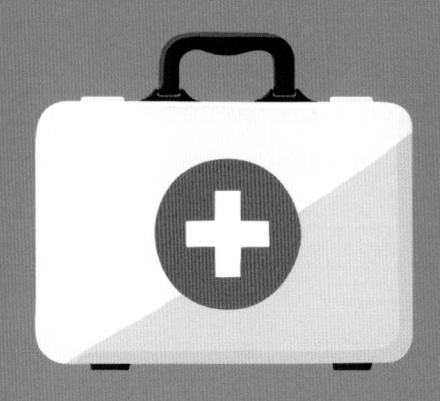

Do you know first aid?
Connaissez-vous les gestes de premiers secours?

(kon-ess-ay-voo lay jhest duh prem-ee-air suh-cor)

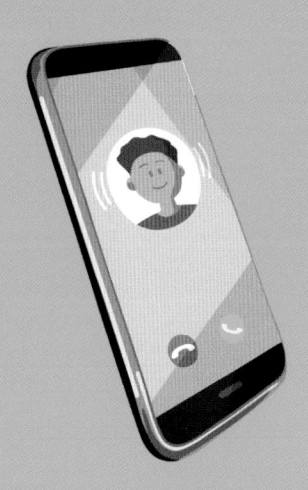

Do you have a cell phone?
Avez vous un portable?

(a-vay voo uh por-ta-bluh)

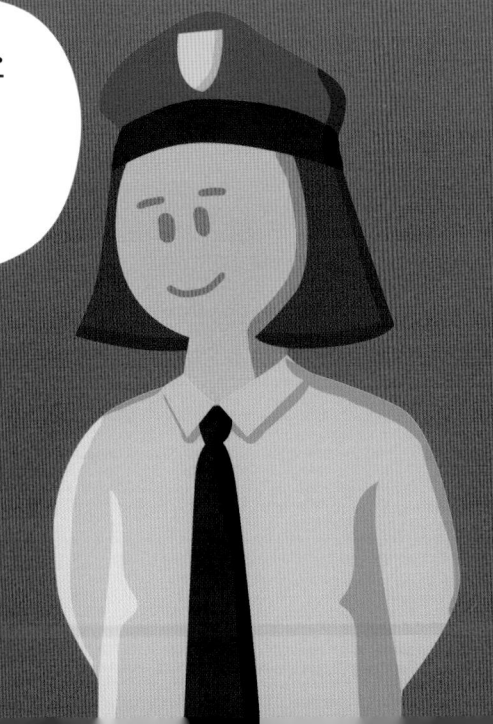

Can you help me? I'm lost.
Pouvez-vous m'aider?
Je suis perdu.

(poo-vay-voo may-day jhuh swee pair-doo)

31

Are you OK?
Ça va?
(sa va)

I have lost …
J'ai perdu …
(jhay pair-doo)

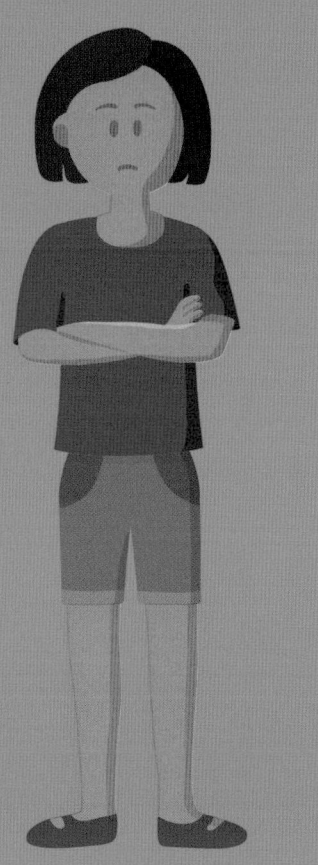

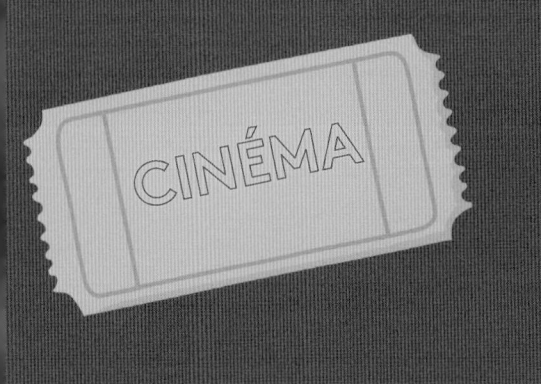

my ticket
mon billet

(mon bee-yay)

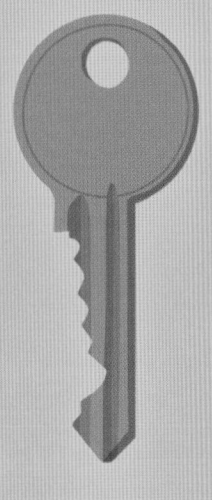

my key
ma clé

(ma klay)

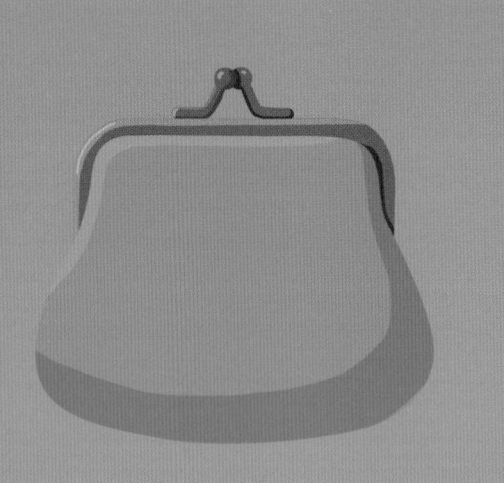

my purse
mon porte-monnaie

(mon port-mo-nay)

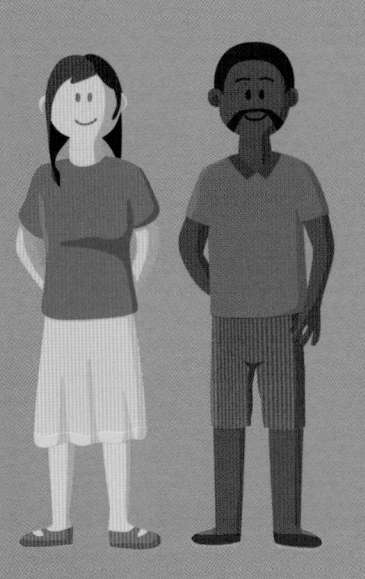

my parents
mes parents

(may pa-ron)

Where am I?
Où suis-je?
(oo swee-jh)

Where is .../Where are ...
Où est .../Où sont ...
(oo eh/oo sohn)

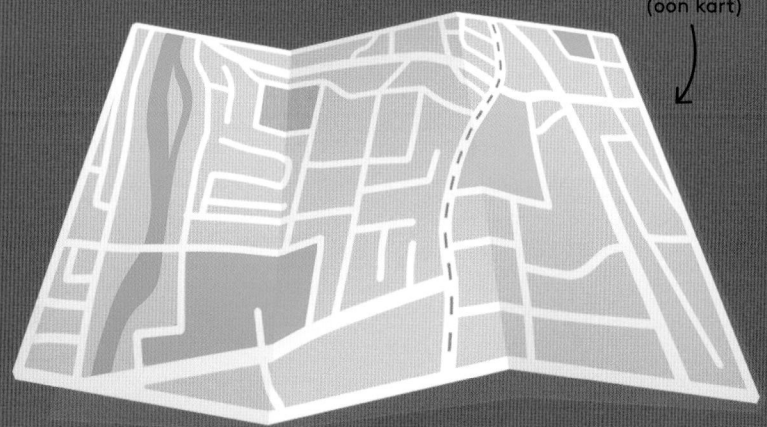

map
une carte
(oon kart)

Do you have a map?
Avez-vous une carte?
(a-vay-voo oon kart)

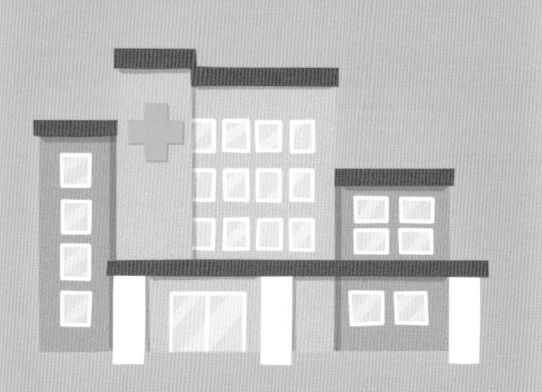

the hospital?

l'hôpital?

(lo-pee-tal)

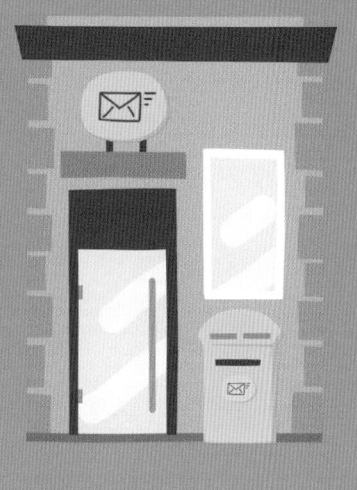

the post office?

le bureau de poste?

(luh bew-roh duh po-st)

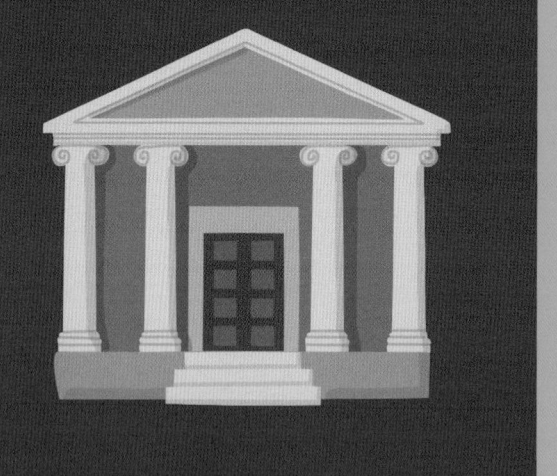

the bank?

la banque?

(la bong-k)

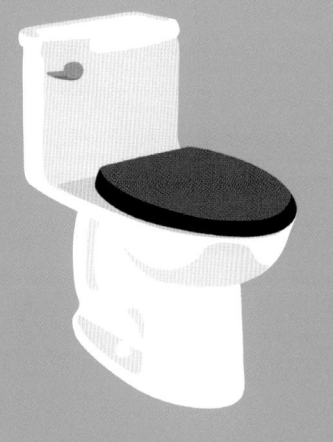

the nearest restroom?

les toilettes les plus proches?

(lay twa-let lay ploo prosh)

It's over there!
C'est là-bas!

(seh la-ba)

I don't know.
Je ne sais pas.

(jhuh nuh say pa)

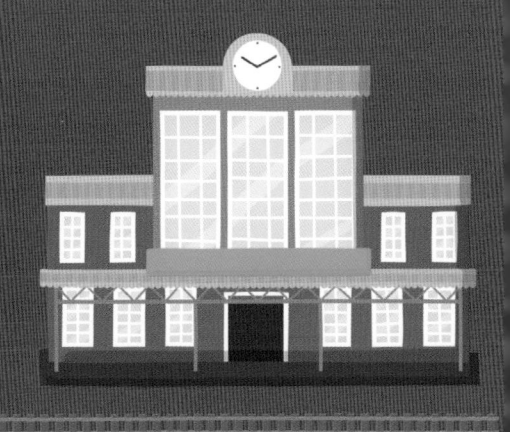

It's next to the train station.
C'est à côté de la gare.

(seh a coh-tay duh la gar)

Is it a long way?
C'est loin?

(seh lwan)

It will take ten minutes.
Ça va prendre dix minutes.

(sa va pron-dr dees min-oot)

It's not far.
Ce n'est pas loin.

(se nay pa lwan)

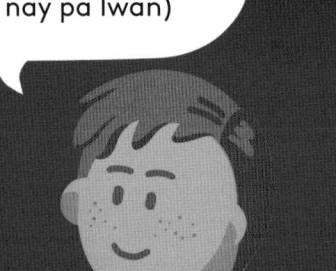

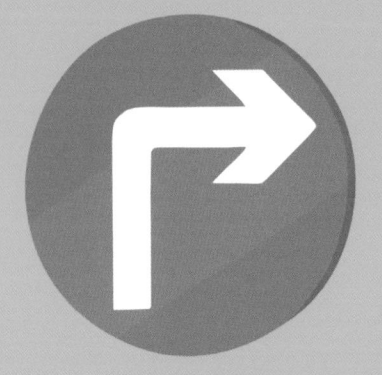

Turn right.
Tournez à droite.

(tuhr-nay a dwat)

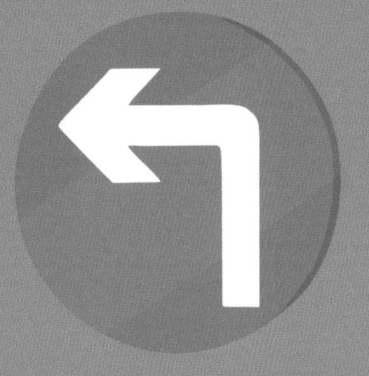

Turn left.
Tournez à gauche.

(tuhr-nay a goh-sh)

Go straight ahead ...
Continuez tout droit ...

(kon-tin-oo-ay toot dwa)

at the traffic lights
aux feux

(oh fuh)

at the traffic circle
au rond-point

(oh ron-pwah)

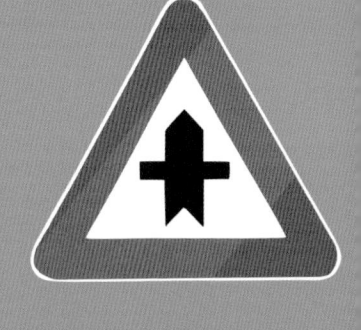

at the crossroads
au carrefour

(oh kar-for)

Where are you going?
Où allez-vous?

(oo a-lay-voo)

We are going …
Nous allons …

(nooz a-lonz)

bus
un autobus
(uhn o-toh-boos)

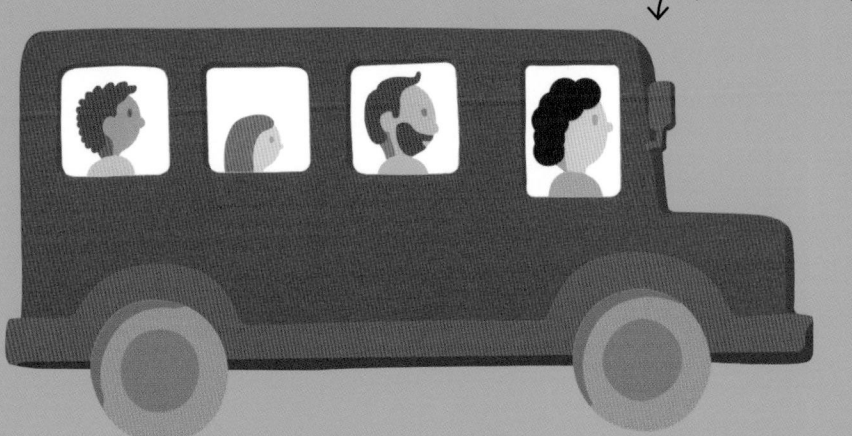

Can I come with you?
Puis-je venir avec vous?

(pwee-jhuh vuh-neer a-vek voo)

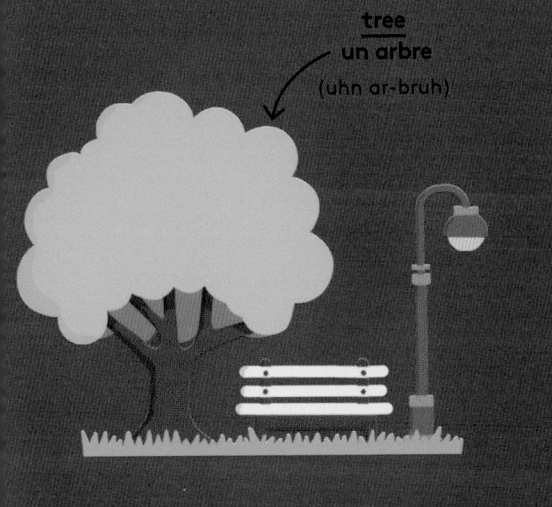

tree
un arbre
(uhn ar-bruh)

to the park
au parc

(oh park)

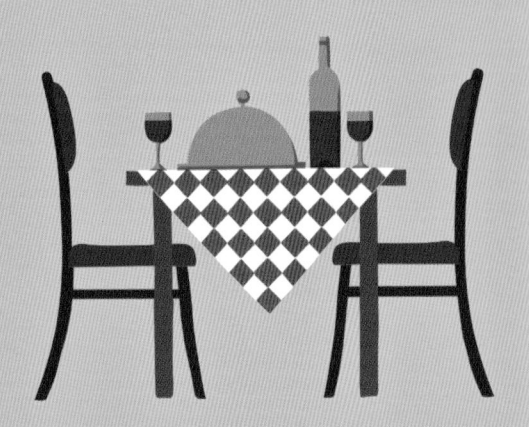

to the restaurant
au restaurant

(oh res-toh-ron)

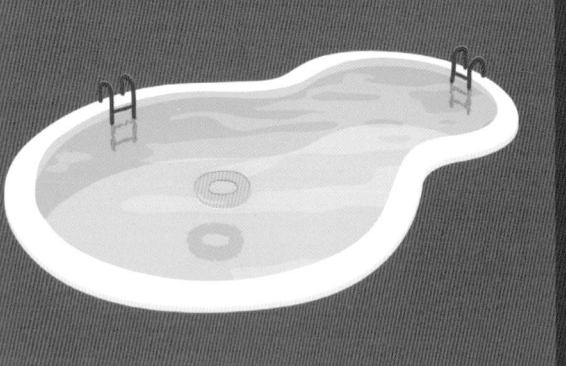

to the swimming pool
à la piscine

(a la pee-seen)

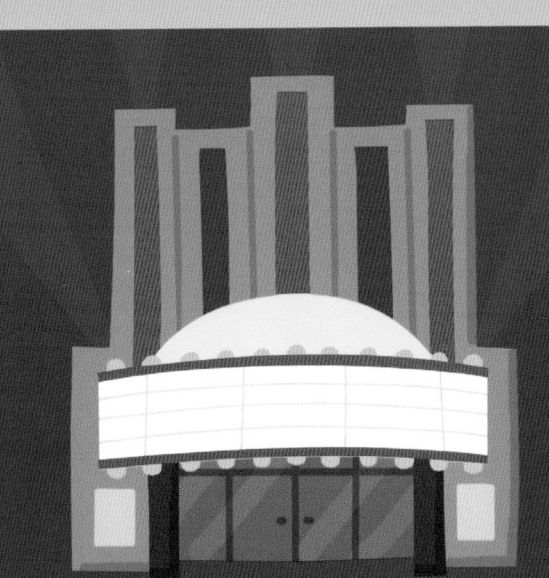

to the movie theater
au cinéma

(oh see-nay-ma)

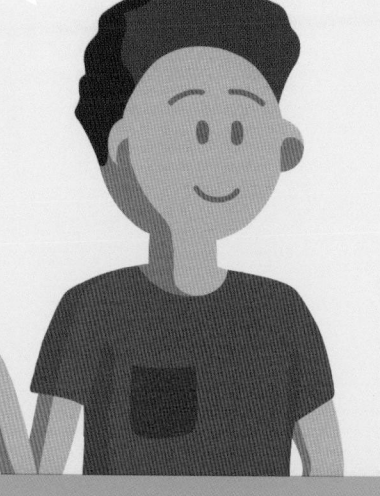

Let's go shopping!
Allons aux magasins!

(a-lonz oh ma-ga-zan)

Good idea!
Bonne idée!

(bon ee-day)

SUPERMARCHÉ

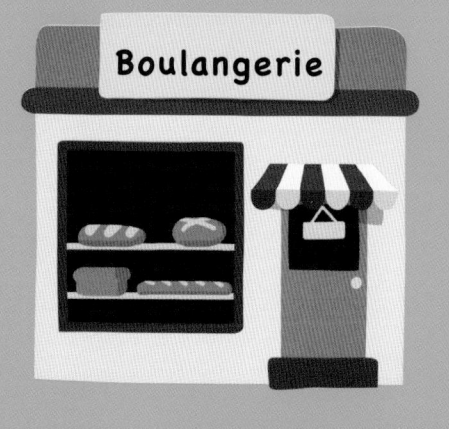

Boulangerie

at the supermarket
au supermarché

(oh soo-pair-mar-shay)

at the bakery
à la boulangerie

(a la boo-lon-jher-ee)

40

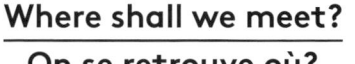

Where shall we meet?
On se retrouve où?

(on suh ruh-troov oo)

I'll meet you ...
Je te retrouve ...

(jhuh tuh ruh-troov)

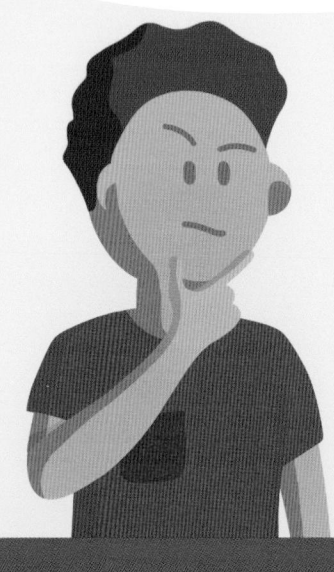

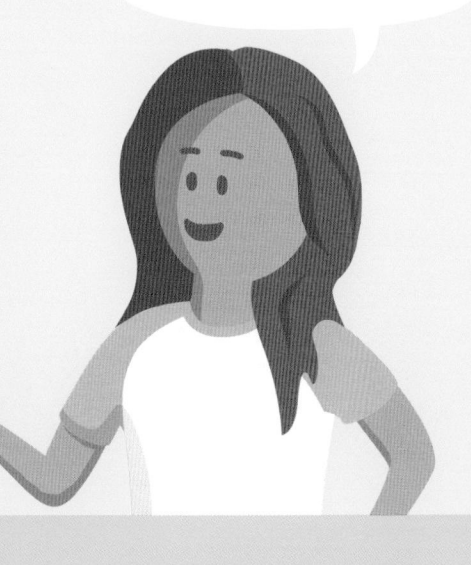

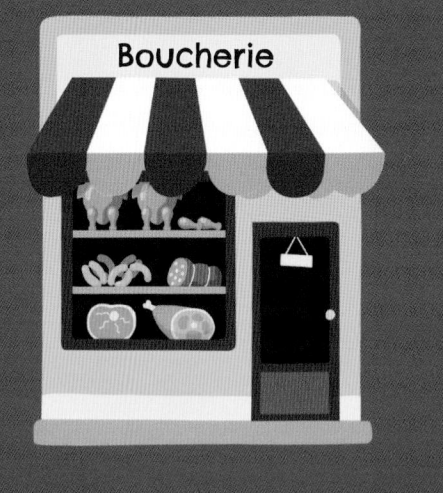

at the butcher
à la boucherie

(a la boo-shair-ee)

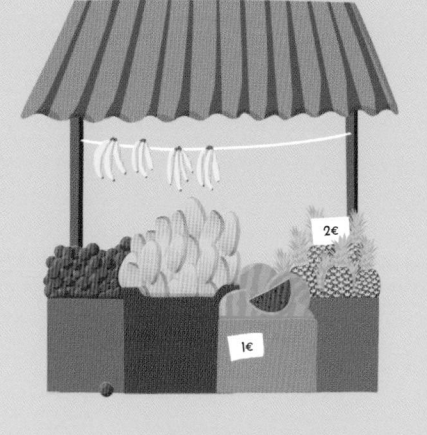

at the market
au marché

(oh mar-shay)

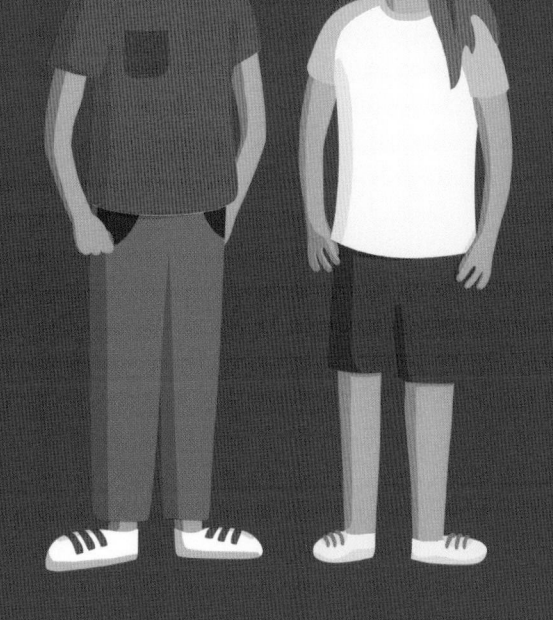

Boulangerie

OUVERT

It's open.
C'est ouvert.
(seh oo-vair)

Is it open?
Est-ce que c'est ouvert?
(es kuh seh oo-vair)

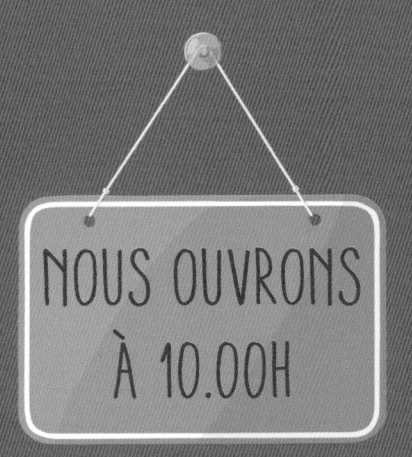

It's closed.
C'est fermé.

(seh fair-may)

It opens at ten o'clock.
On ouvre à dix heures.

(on oov-r a dees uhr)

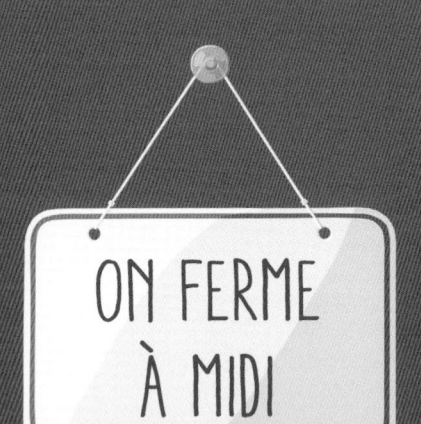

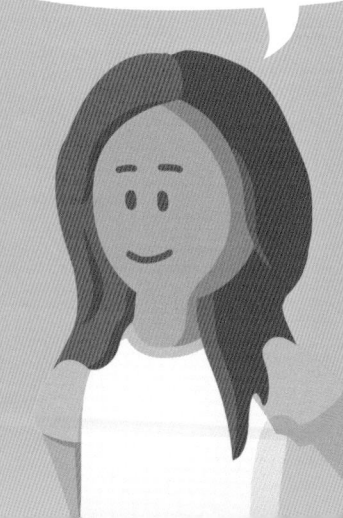

Let's go somewhere else.
Allons ailleurs.

(a-lon aye-uhr)

It closes at midday.
On ferme à midi.

(on fairm a mi-dee)

I would like to buy …
Je voudrais acheter …
(jhuh voo-dray ash-tay)

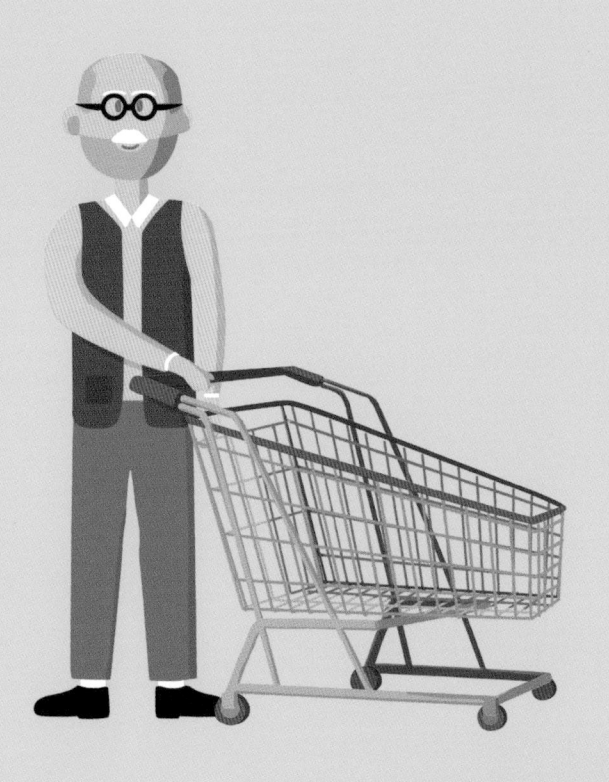

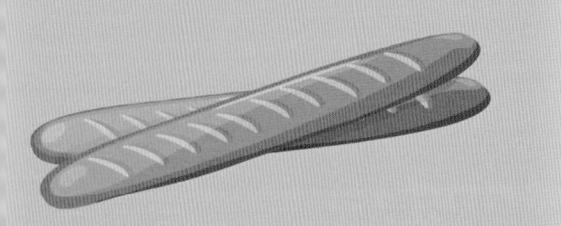

some bread
du pain

(doo pan)

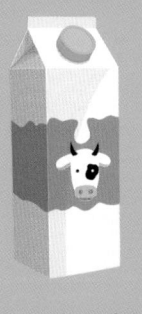

some milk
du lait

(doo lay)

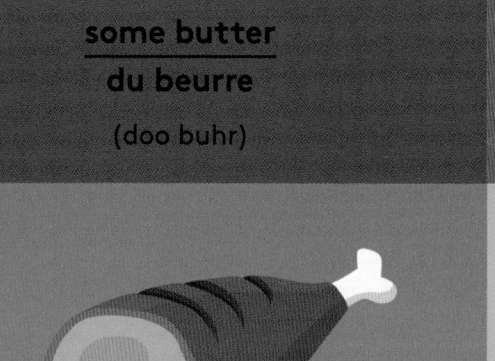

some butter
du beurre

(doo buhr)

some cheese
du fromage

(doo fro-ma-jh)

some ham
du jambon

(doo jhom-bon)

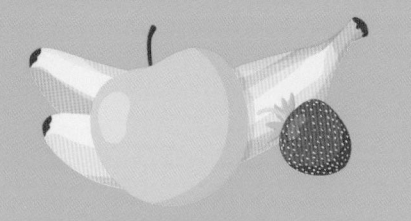

some fruit
des fruits

(day fwee)

45

Did you bring ...
As-tu apporté ...
(a-too a-por-tay)

the shopping list?
la liste des courses?

(la leest day kors)

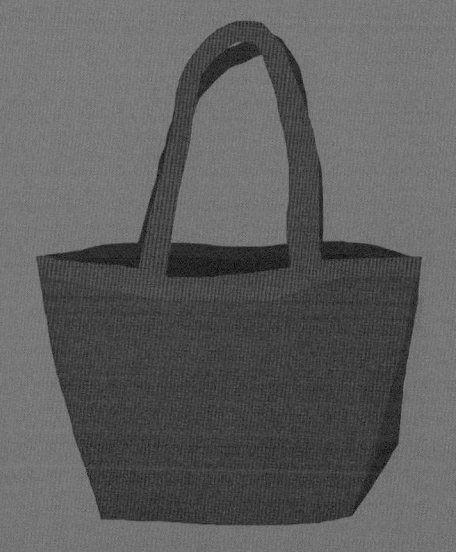

a shopping bag?
un sac de courses?

(uh sak duh kors)

46

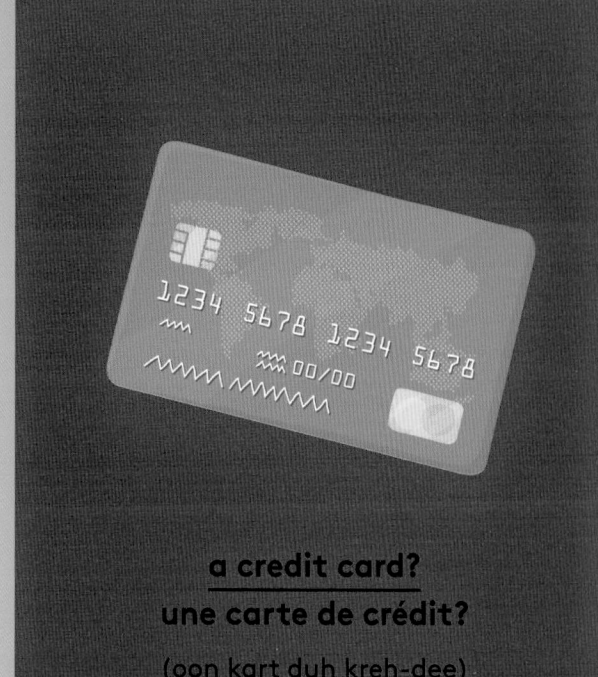

some money?
de l'argent?

(duh lar-jhon)

a credit card?
une carte de crédit?

(oon kart duh kreh-dee)

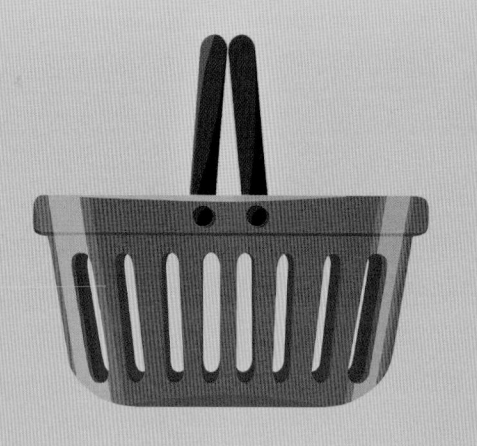

Here's a basket.
Voici un panier.

(vwa-see uh pan-yay)

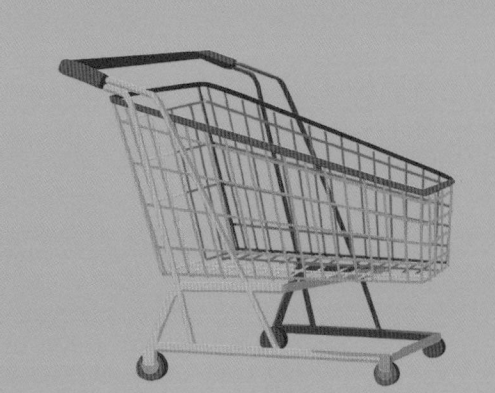

I'll push the shopping cart.
Je vais pousser le chariot.

(jhuh vay poo-say luh sha-ree-oh)

Do you have …
Avez-vous …
(a-vay-voo)

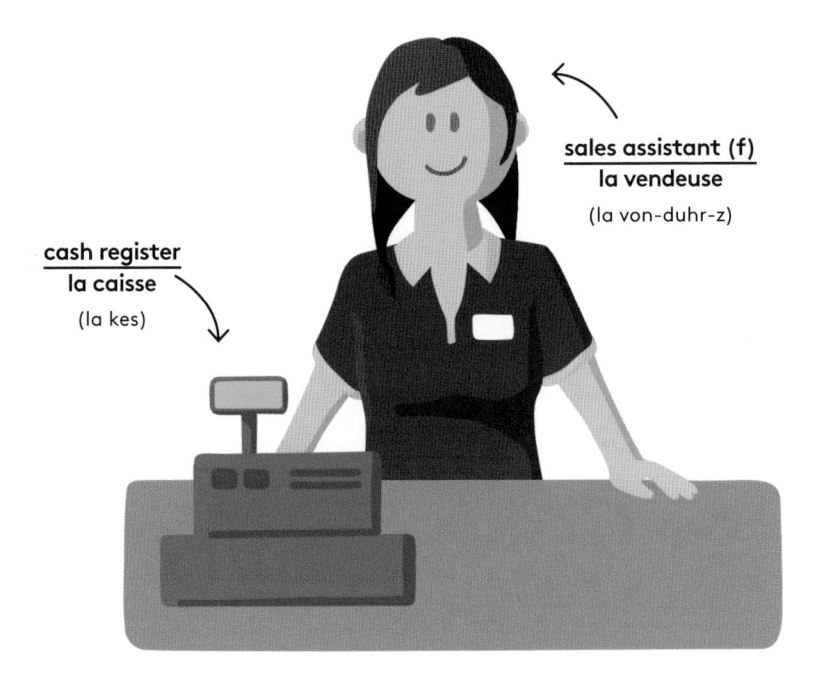

sales assistant (f)
la vendeuse
(la von-duhr-z)

cash register
la caisse
(la kes)

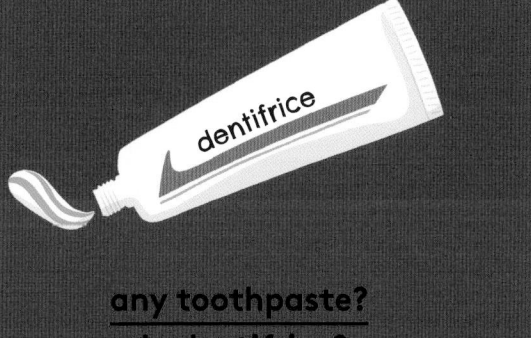

any toothpaste?
du dentifrice?

(doo don-tee-frees)

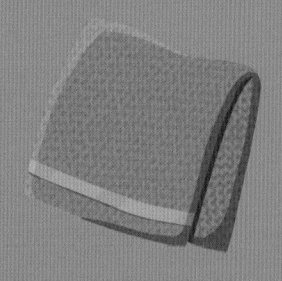

a washcloth?
un gant de toilette?

(uh gant duh twa-let)

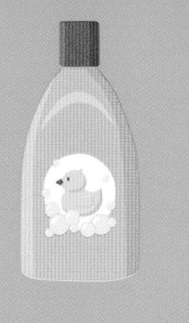

any shampoo?
du shampooing?

(doo shom-pwan)

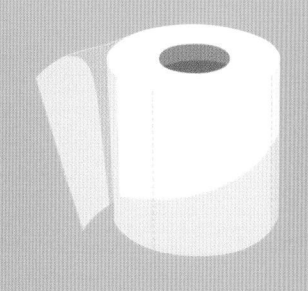

any toilet paper?
du papier hygiénique?

(doo pap-ee-yay ee-jhee-en-eek)

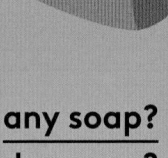

any soap?
du savon?

(doo sa-von)

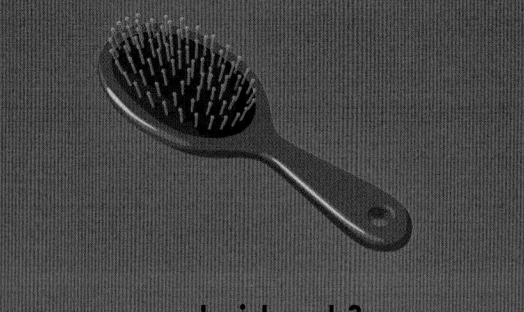

a hairbrush?
une brosse à cheveux?

(oon bross a shuh-vuh)

49

50

**How many
... would you like?
Combien ... voulez-vous?**

(kom-bee-an ... voo-lay-voo)

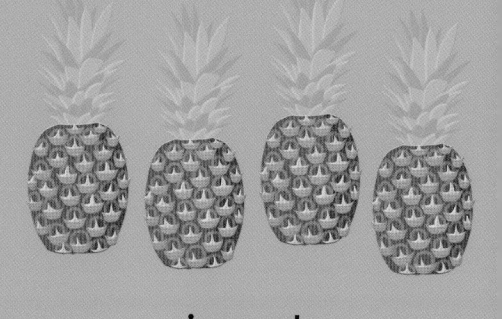

**pineapples
d'ananas**

(da-na-nas)

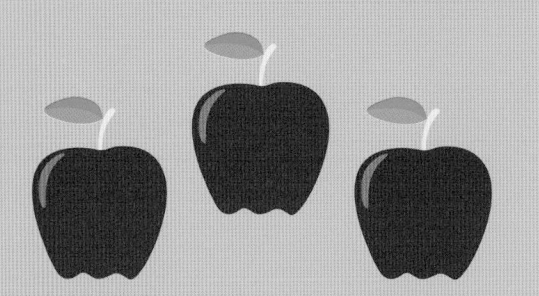

**apples
de pommes**

(duh pom)

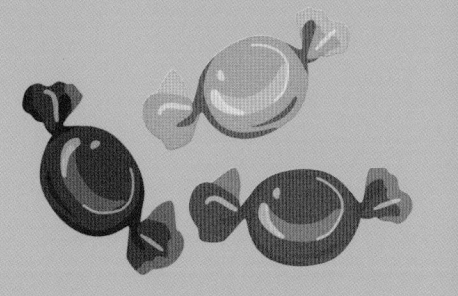

**candies
de bonbons**

(duh bon-bon)

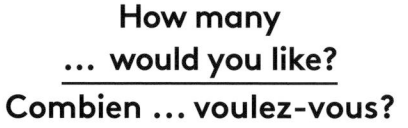

**croissants
de croissants**

(duh kwa-son)

**I would like three please.
J'en voudrais trois
s'il vous plaît.**

(jhon voo-dray twah seel voo pleh)

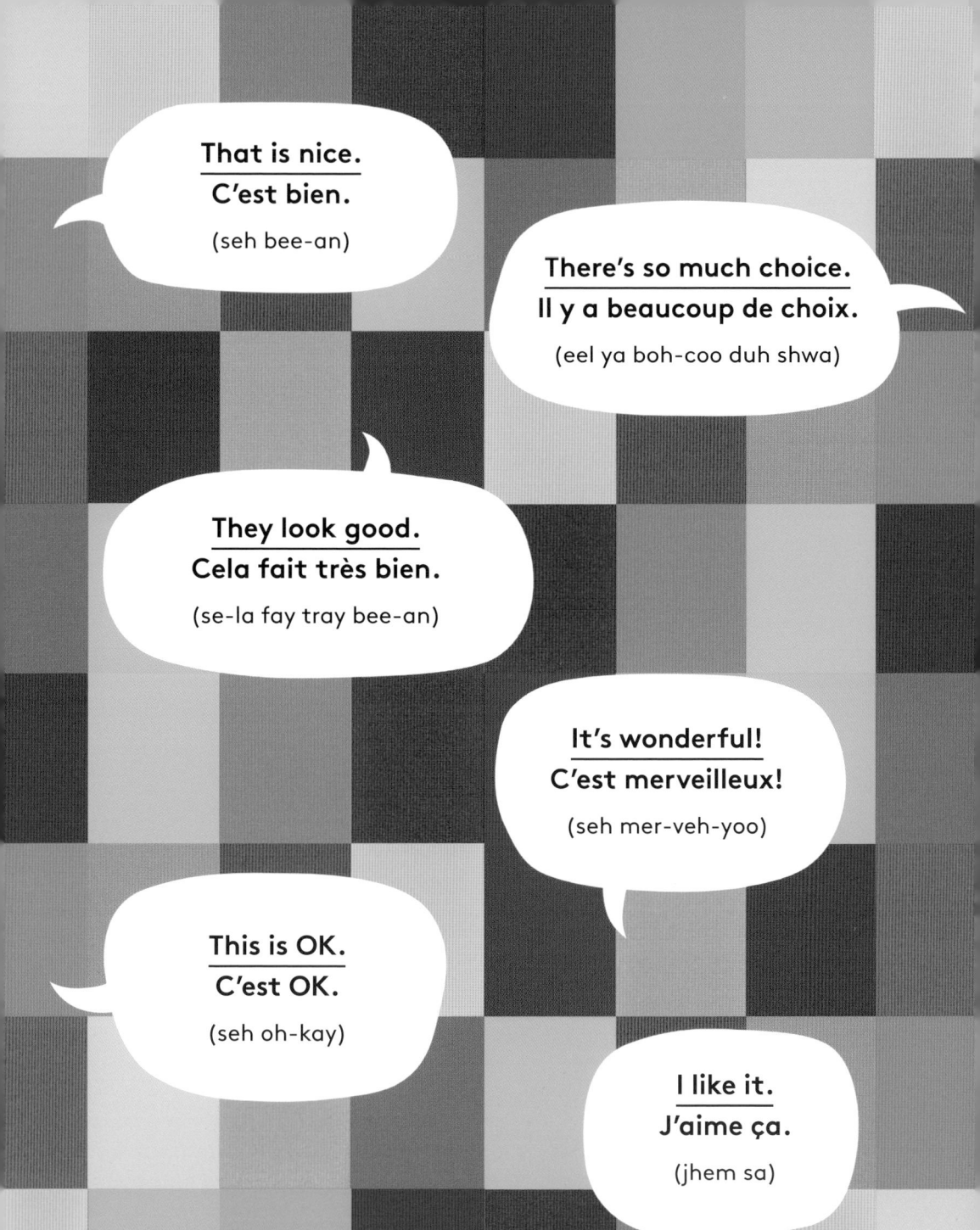

That is nice.
C'est bien.
(seh bee-an)

There's so much choice.
Il y a beaucoup de choix.
(eel ya boh-coo duh shwa)

They look good.
Cela fait très bien.
(se-la fay tray bee-an)

It's wonderful!
C'est merveilleux!
(seh mer-veh-yoo)

This is OK.
C'est OK.
(seh oh-kay)

I like it.
J'aime ça.
(jhem sa)

51

How much is …
Combien coûte …
(kom-bee-an koot)

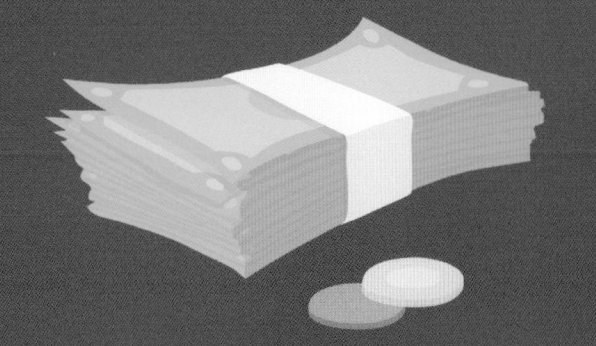

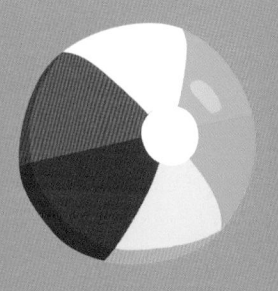

the beach ball?
le ballon de plage?

(luh ba-lon duh pla-jh)

the notepad?
le cahier?

(luh ka-yeh)

stamp
un timbre

(uh tam-bruh)

the postcard?
la carte postale?

(la kart poh-stal)

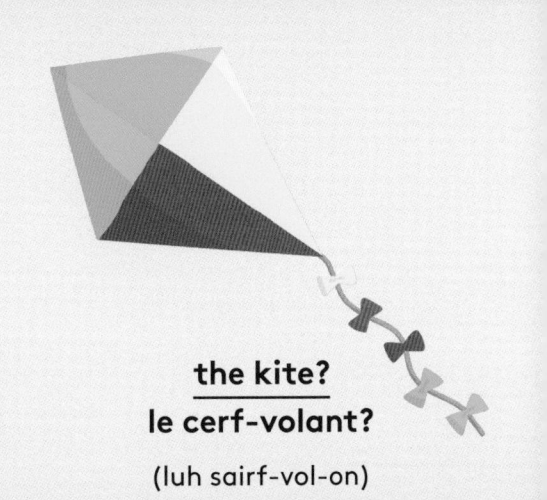

the kite?
le cerf-volant?

(luh sairf-vol-on)

the bucket?
le seau?

(luh so)

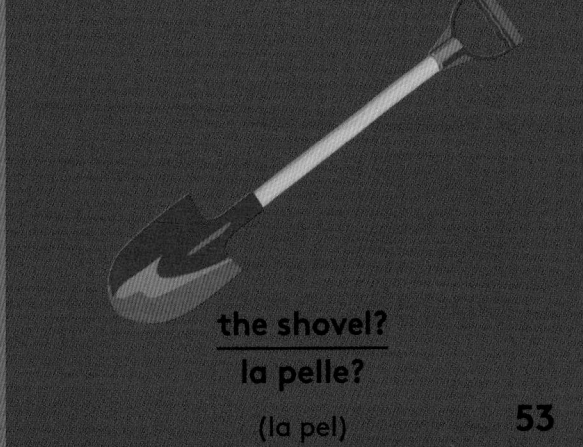

the shovel?
la pelle?

(la pel)

53

How much are …
Combien coûtent …
(kom-bee-an koot)

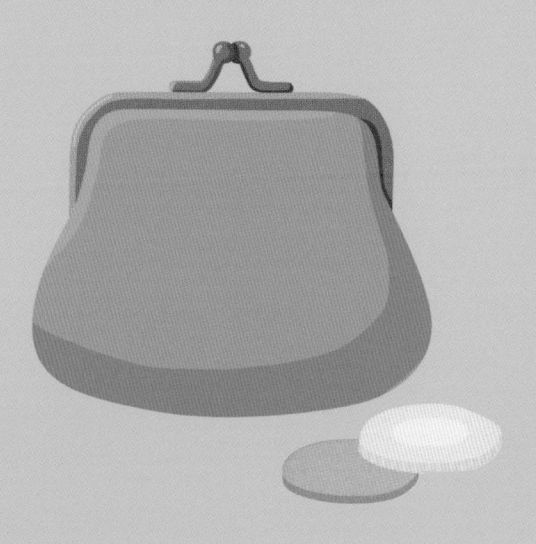

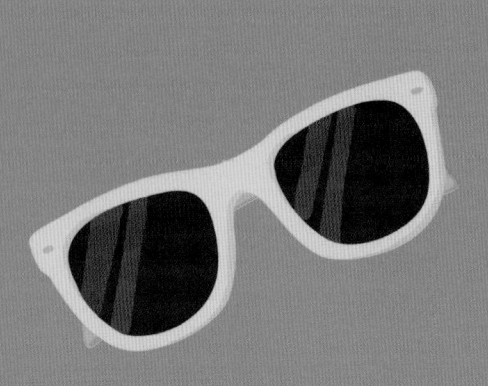

the sunglasses?
les lunettes de soleil?

(lay loo-net duh soh-lay)

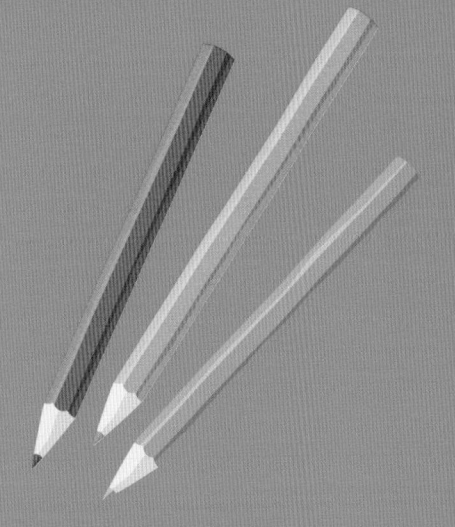

the pencils?
les crayons?

(lay kray-on)

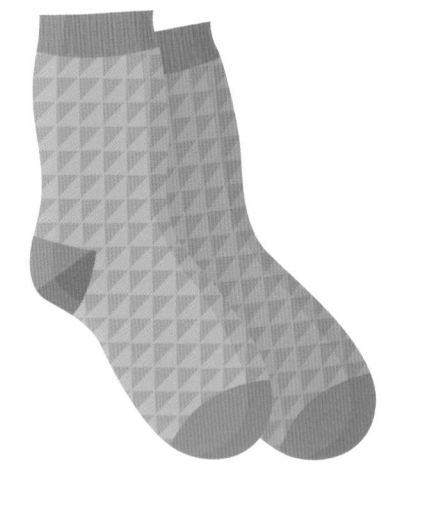

the socks?
les chaussettes?

(lay show-set)

the flowers?
les fleurs?

(lay fluhr)

55

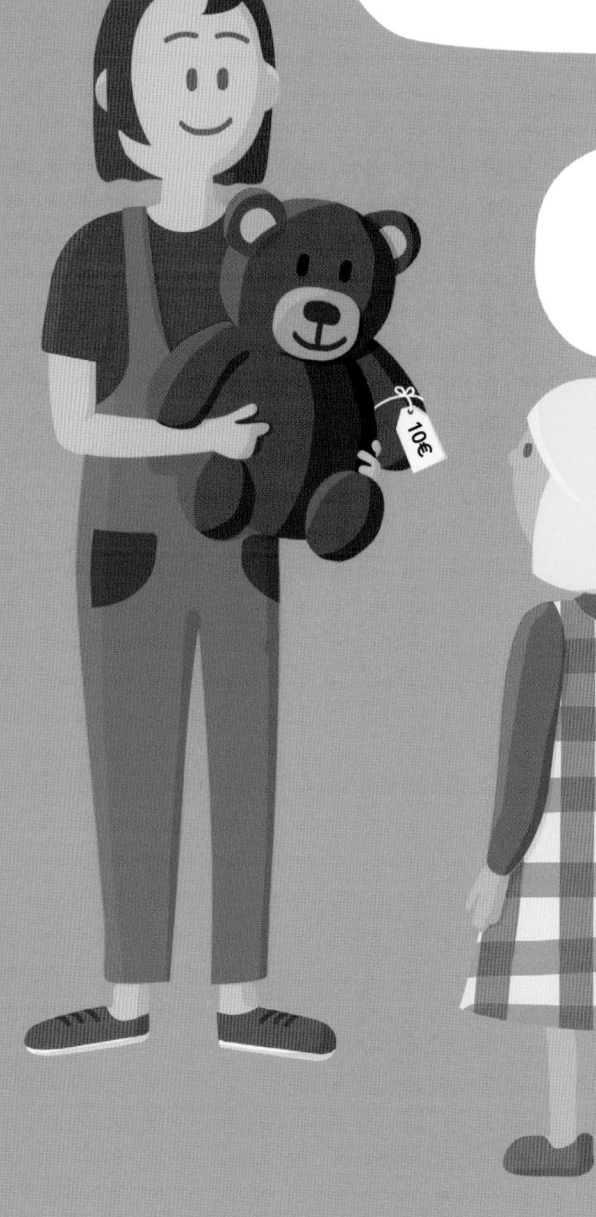

This is ten euros.
Ça coûte dix euros.
(sa coot dees uh-roh)

I'll take it!
Je vais le prendre!
(jhuh vay luh pron-dr)

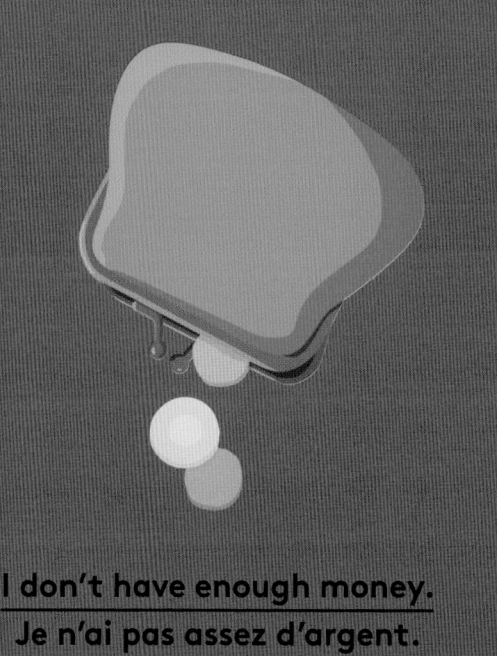

I don't have enough money.
Je n'ai pas assez d'argent.

(jhuh nay pa ass-ay dar-jhon)

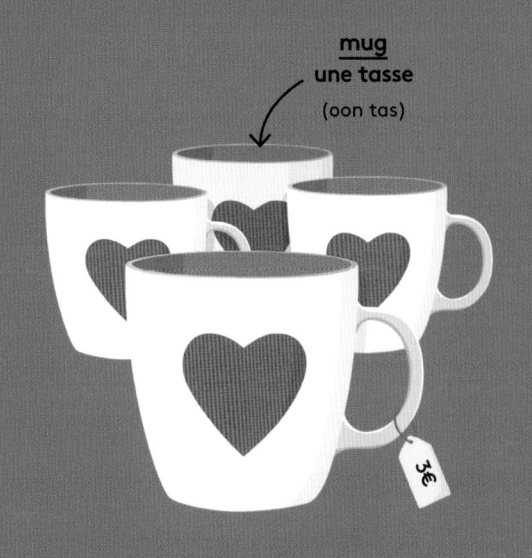

mug
une tasse
(oon tas)

3€

I just want one.
J'en veux juste un (m) / une (f).

(jhon vuh jhoost uh / oon)

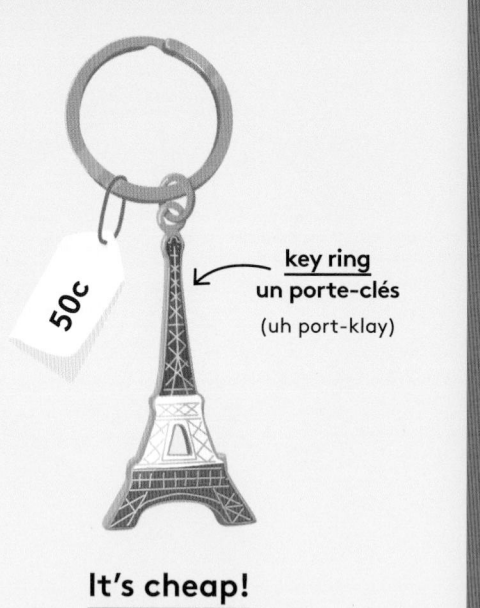

50c

key ring
un porte-clés
(uh port-klay)

It's cheap!
Ce n'est pas cher!

(suh nay pa shair)

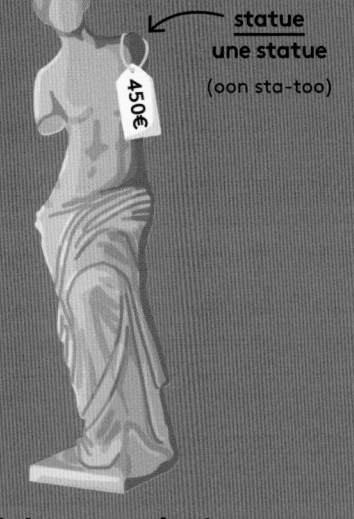

statue
une statue
(oon sta-too)

450€

It's expensive!
C'est cher!

(seh shair)

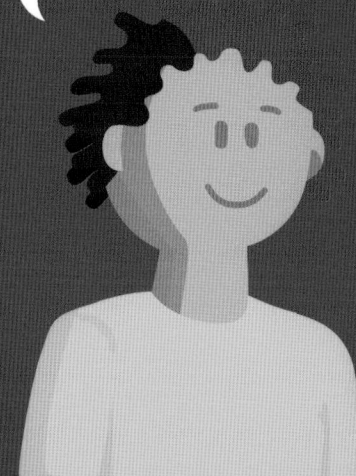

What's the time?
Quelle heure est-il?

(kel uhr et-eel)

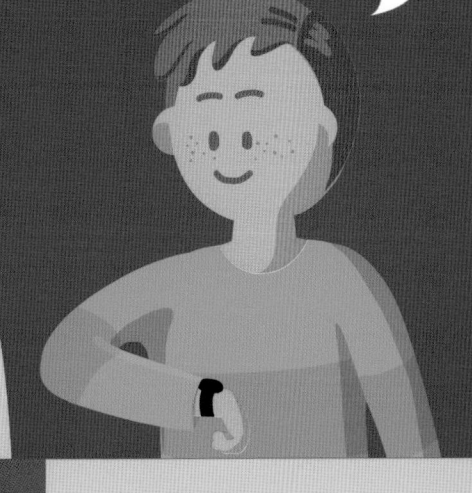

The time is ...
Il est ...

(eel eh)

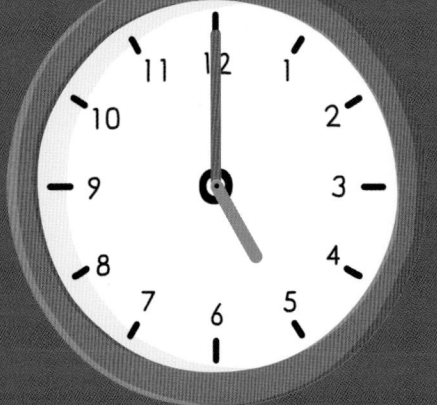

clock
une horloge
(oon oh-lerjh)

five o'clock
cinq heures
(sank uhr)

a quarter after five
cinq heures et quart
(sank uhr eh kar)

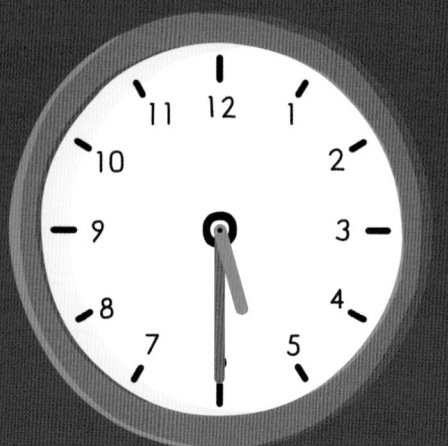

half past five
cinq heures et demie

(sank uhr eh duh-mee)

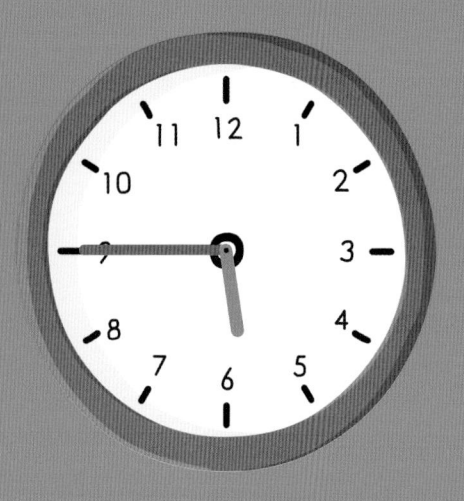

a quarter of six
six heures moins le quart

(sees uhr mwan luh kar)

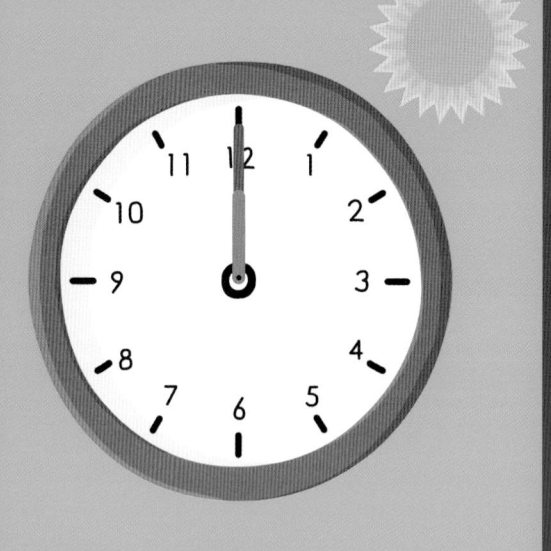

midday
midi

(mi-dee)

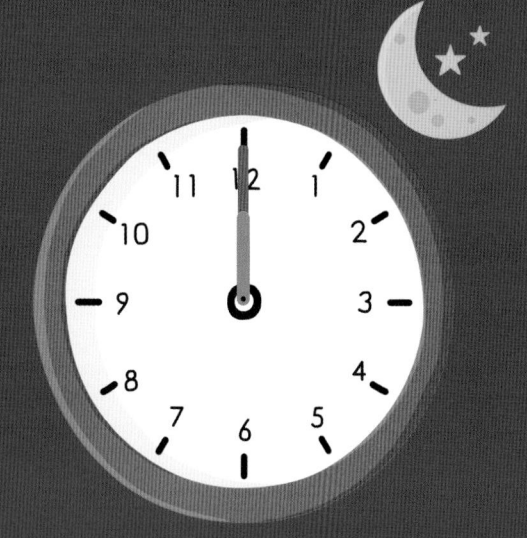

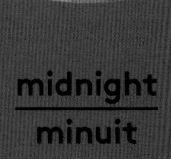

midnight
minuit

(min-wee)

morning
le matin
(luh ma-tah)

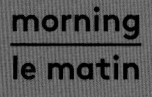

afternoon
l'après-midi
(la-pray-mee-dee)

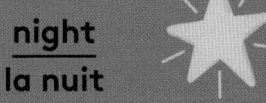

evening
le soir
(luh swar)

night
la nuit
(la nwee)

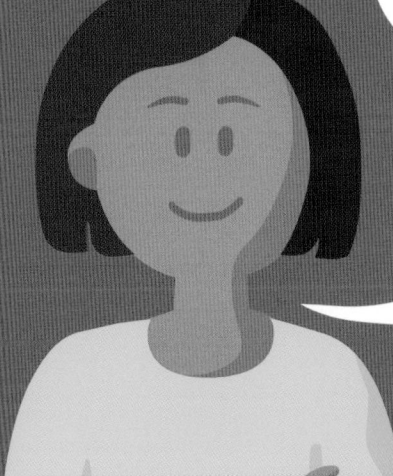

What time do you get up?
À quelle heure tu te lèves?
(a kel uhr too tuh lev)

I get up at a quarter after six.
Je me lève à six heures et quart.
(jhuh muh lev a sees uhr eh kar)

What time do you go to school?
À quelle heure vas-tu à l'école?

(a kel uhr va-too a leh-kol)

I go to school at half past eight.
Je vais à l'école à huit heures et demie.

(jhuh vay a leh-kol a hweet uhr
ay duh-mee)

When do you go to bed?
À quelle heure tu te couches?

(a kel uhr too tuh koo-sh)

That's late!
C'est tard!

(seh tar)

I go to bed at ten o'clock.
Je me couche à
vingt-deux heures.

(jhuh muh koo-sh a
van-duhz uhr)

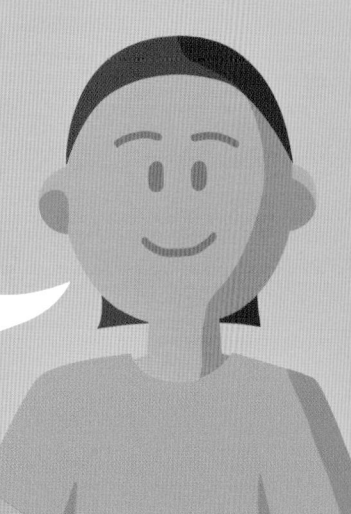
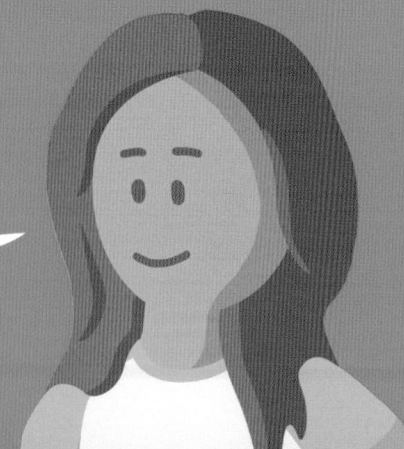

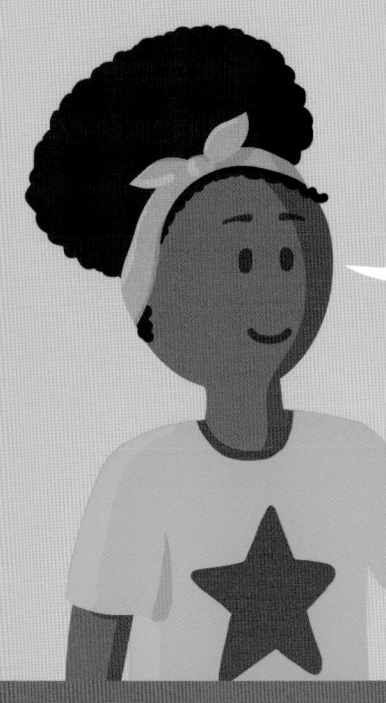

This is ...
Voici ...

(vwa-see)

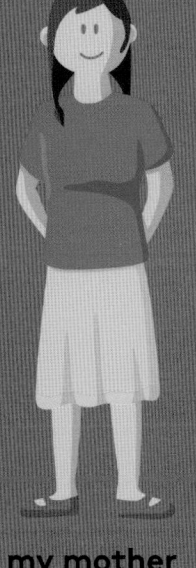

my mother
ma mère

(ma mair)

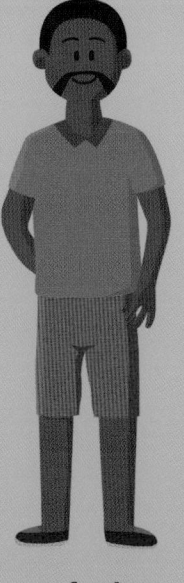

my father
mon père

(mon pair)

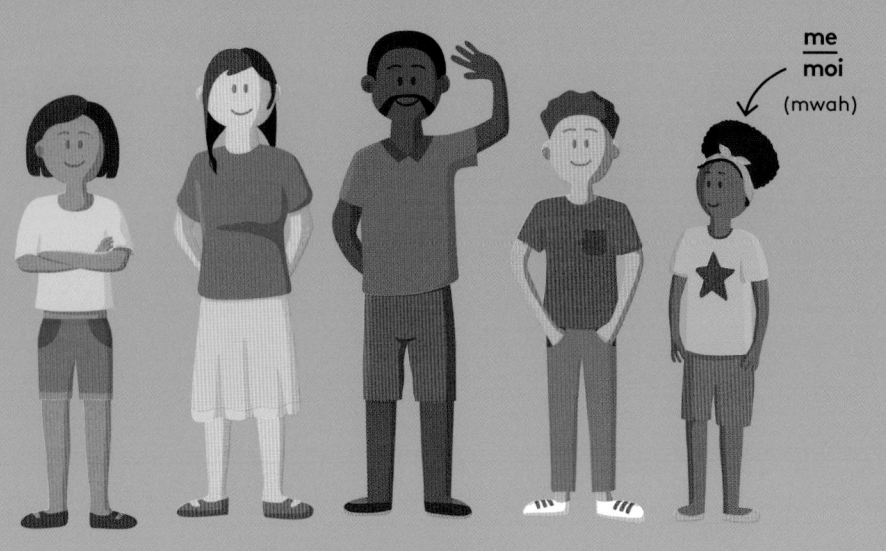

me
moi
(mwah)

my family
ma famille

(ma fam-ee)

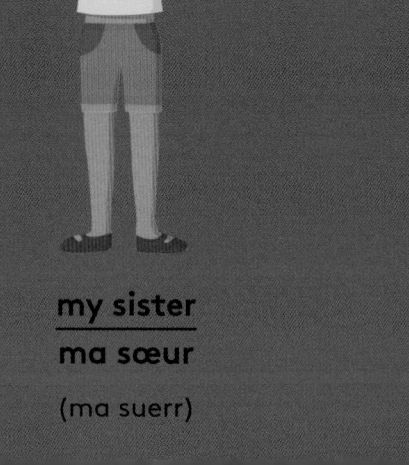

my sister
ma sœur

(ma suerr)

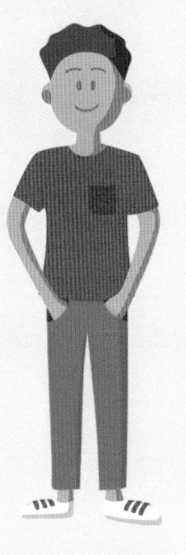

my brother
mon frère

(mon frair)

"Who's this?" and "Who's that?" are the same in French!

Who's this?
Qui est-ce?

(kee es)

Is this ...
Est-ce que c'est ...
(es kuh seh)

Who's that?
Qui est-ce?

(kee es)

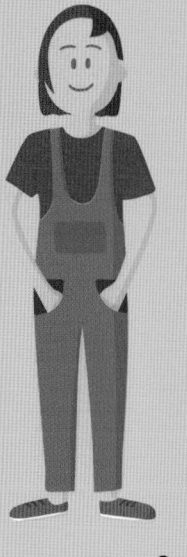

your aunt?
ta tante?

(ta tont)

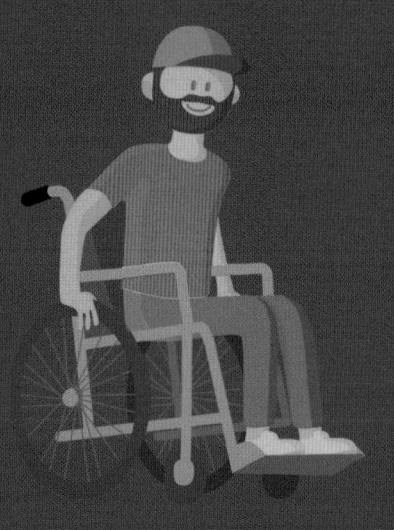

your uncle?
ton oncle?

(ton onk-l)

your grandmother?
ta grandmère?

(ta gron-mair)

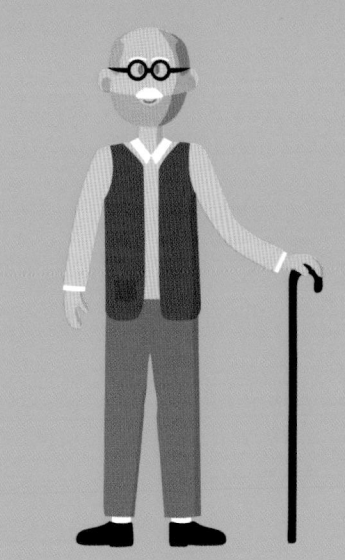

your grandfather?
ton grandpère?

(ton gron-pair)

Are they your cousins?
Est-ce qu'ils sont tes cousins?

(es keel son tay koo-zah)

Yes.
Oui.

(wee)

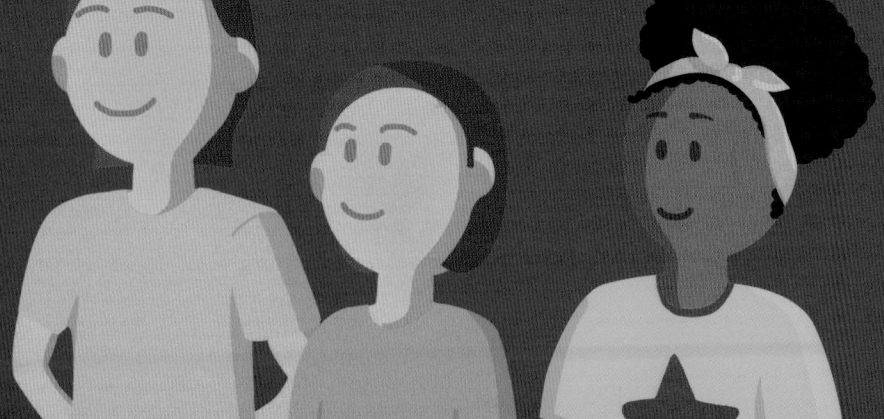

Do you have any brothers or sisters?
As-tu des frères ou des sœurs?

(a-too day frair oo day suerr)

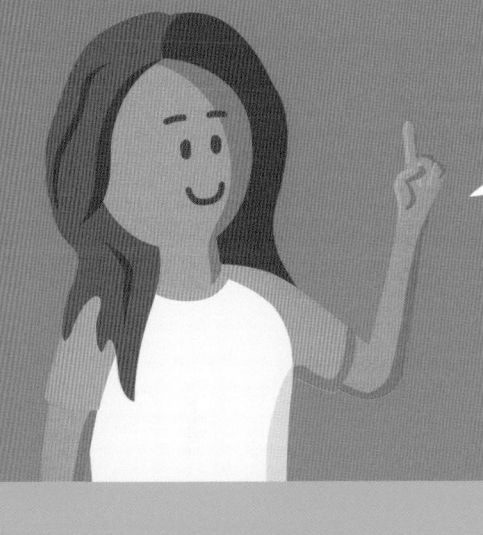

I have one brother.
J'ai un frère.

(jhay uh frair)

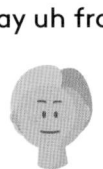

**I have two sisters
and three stepbrothers.**
J'ai deux sœurs et trois demi-frères.

(jhay duh suerr eh twa duh-mee-frair)

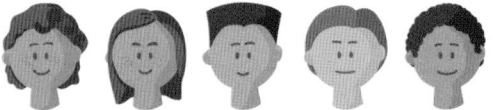

I don't have any brothers or sisters.
Je n'ai pas de frères ou de sœurs.

(jhuh nay pa duh frair oo duh suerr)

I am an only child.
Je suis fille unique (f).

(jhuh swee fee oo-neek)

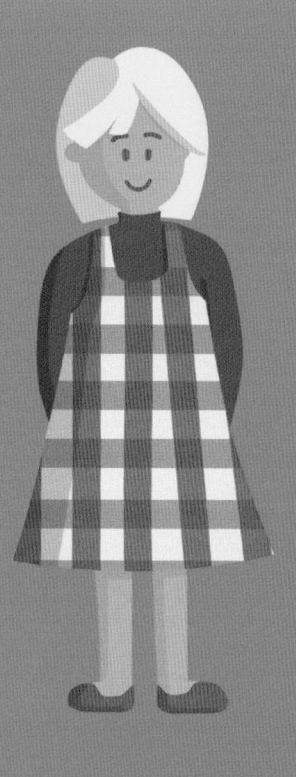

If you are a boy, you say "Je suis fils unique."

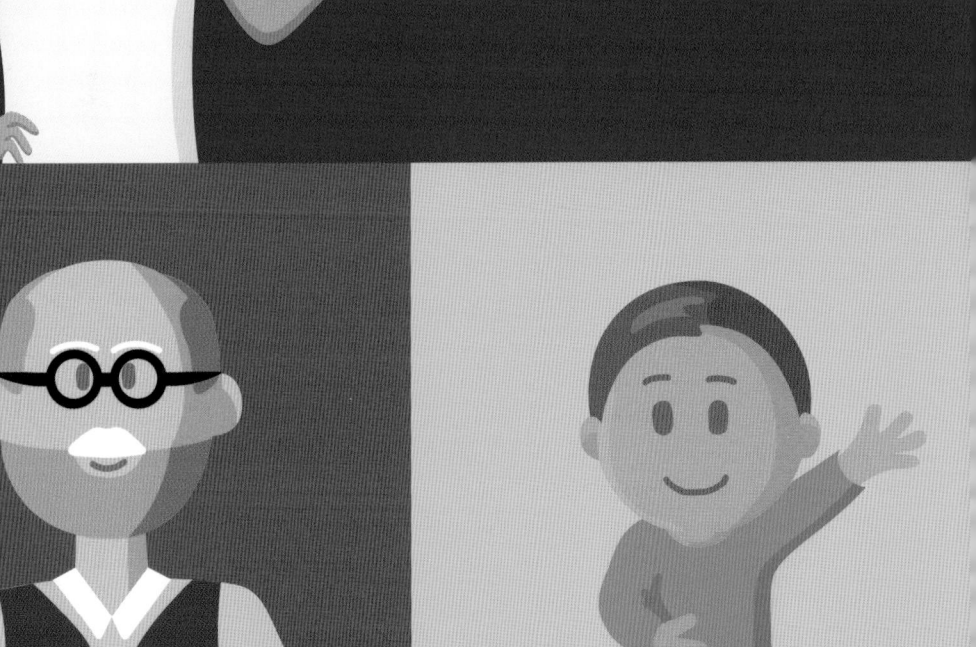

Is your brother older than you?
Est-ce que ton frère est plus âgé que toi?
(es kuh ton frair eh ploo ar-jhay kuh twah)

He is old.
Il est vieux.
(eel eh vee-yuh)

He is young.
Il est jeune.
(eel eh jhuhn)

My brother is younger than me.
Mon frère est plus jeune que moi.

(mon frair eh ploo jhuhn kuh mwah)

**My brother is
older than me.**
**Mon frère est plus
âgé que moi.**

(mon frair eh ploo ar-jhay
kuh mwah)

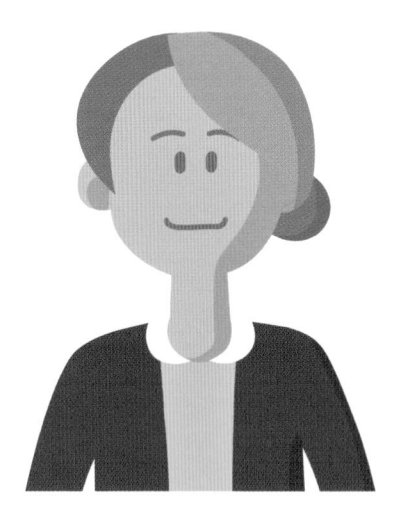

She is old.
Elle est vieille.

(el eh vee-yay)

She is very young!
Elle est très jeune!

(el eh tray jhuhn)

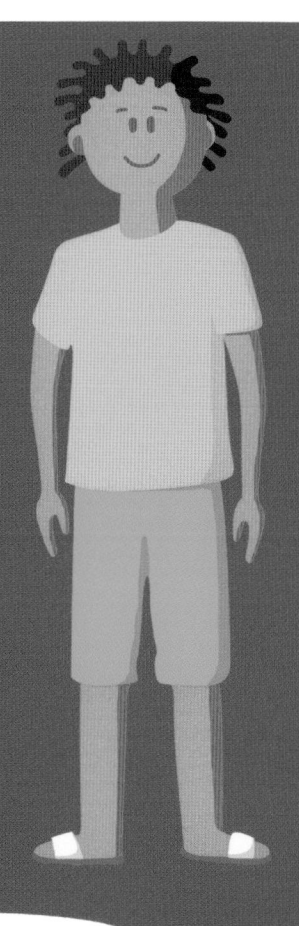

What does your sister look like?
Comment est ta sœur?
(ko-mon eh ta suerr)

Is she tall or short?
Est-ce qu'elle est grande ou petite?
(es kel eh grond oo pteet)

71

She has long hair.
Elle a les cheveux longs.

(el a lay shuh-vuh long)

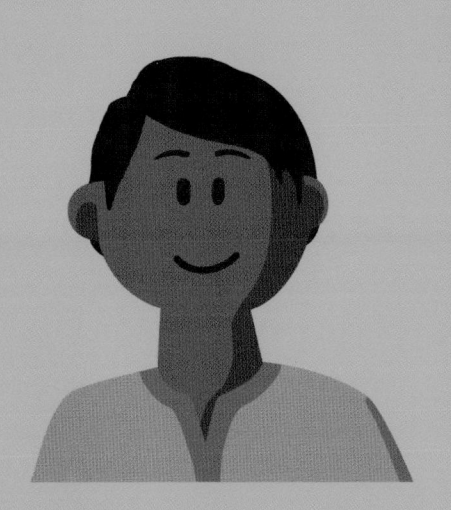

She has short hair.
Elle a les cheveux courts.

(el a lay shuh-vuh kort)

She has straight hair.
Elle a les cheveux raides.

(el a lay shuh-vuh rayd)

She has curly hair.
Elle a les cheveux bouclés.

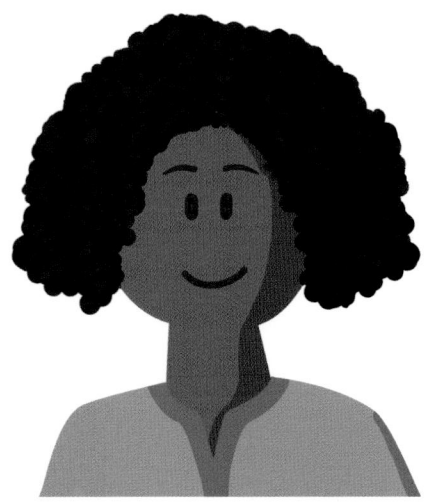

(el a lay shuh-vuh boo-klay)

He has ...
Il a ...
(eel a)

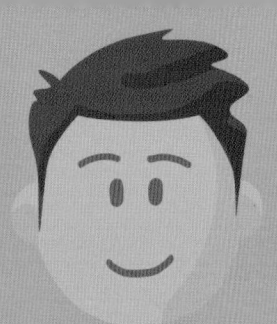

brown hair
les cheveux bruns

(lay shuh-vuh bruhn)

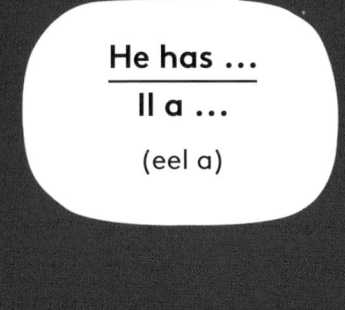

black hair
les cheveux noirs

(lay shuh-vuh nwahr)

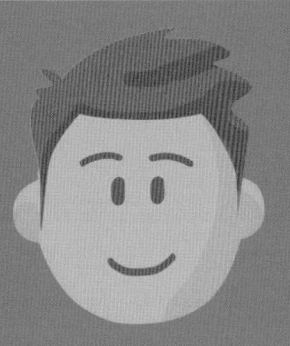

red hair
les cheveux roux

(lay shuh-vuh roo)

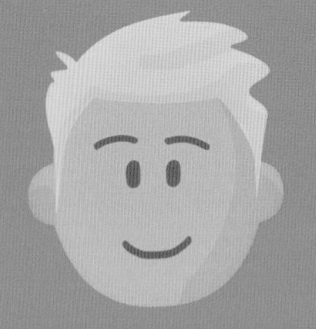

blond hair
les cheveux blonds

(lay shuh-vuh blond)

He has no hair.
Il n'a pas de cheveux.

(eel na pa duh shuh-vuh)

73

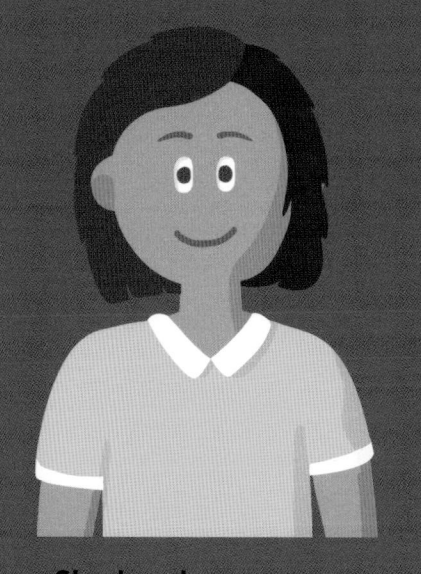

She has brown eyes.
Elle a les yeux bruns.

(el a layz yuh bruhn)

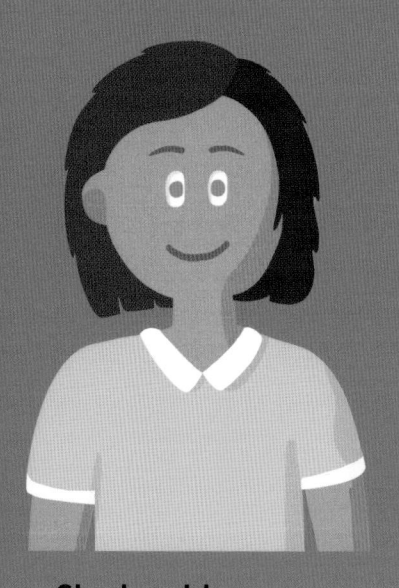

She has blue eyes.
Elle a les yeux bleus.

(el a layz yuh bluh)

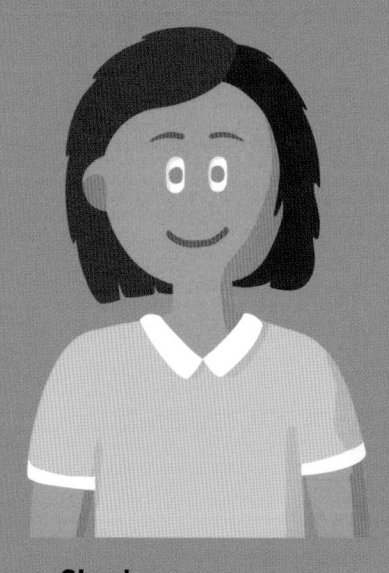

She has gray eyes.
Elle a les yeux gris.

(el a layz yuh gree)

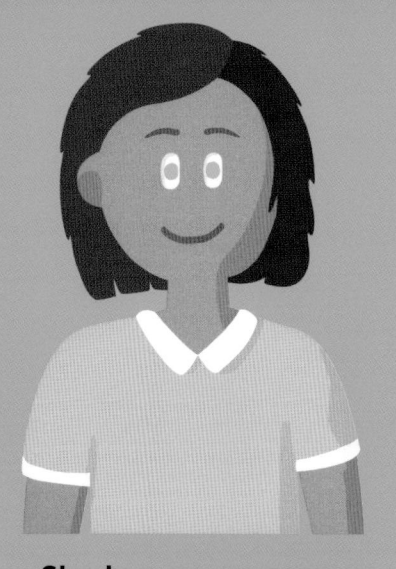

She has green eyes.
Elle a les yeux verts.

(el a layz yuh vair)

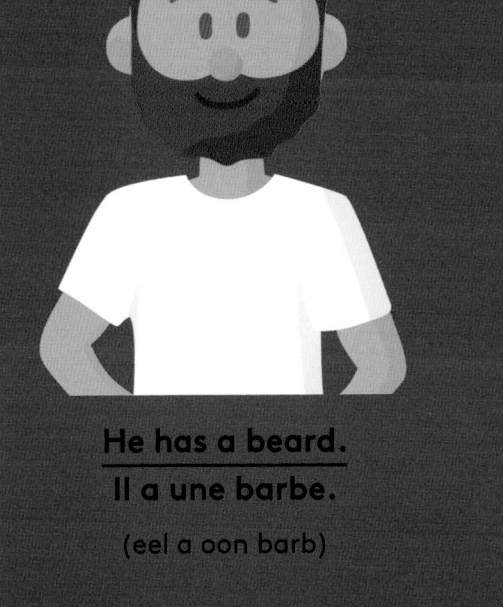

He has a beard.
Il a une barbe.

(eel a oon barb)

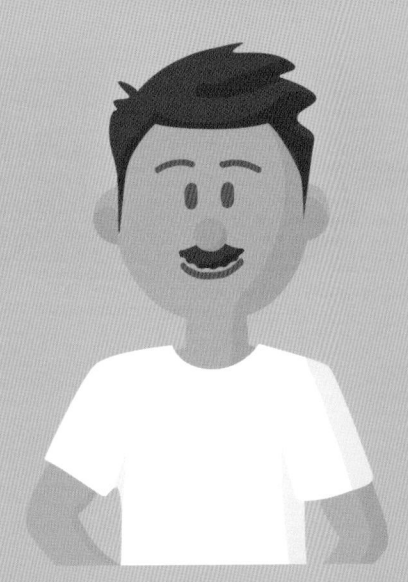

He has a mustache.
Il a une moustache.

(eel a oon moos-tash)

He has freckles.
Il a des taches de rousseur.

(eel a day tash duh roo-suerr)

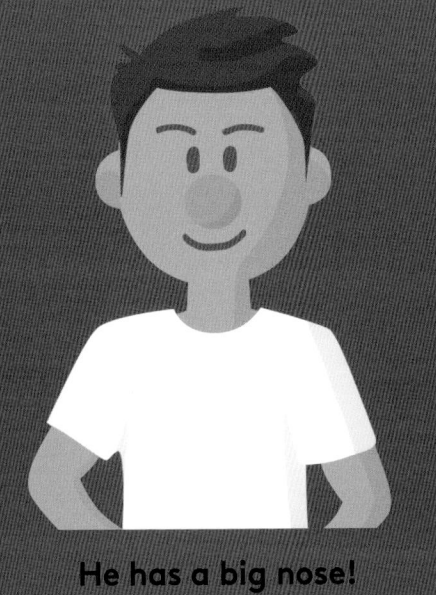

He has a big nose!
Il a un gros nez!

(eel a uh groh neh)

What is he wearing?
Qu'est-ce qu'il porte?

(kes keel port)

In French, most adjectives follow the noun, but some common adjectives come before the noun.

Adjectives describing beauty, age, size, and how good something is usually come before the noun.

He is wearing ...
Il porte ...
(eel port)

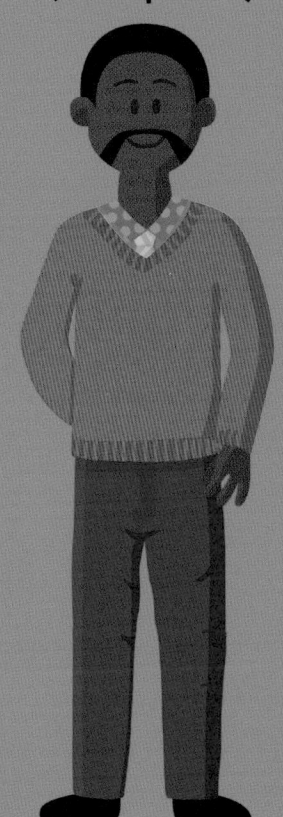

a sweater
un pull
(uh pool)

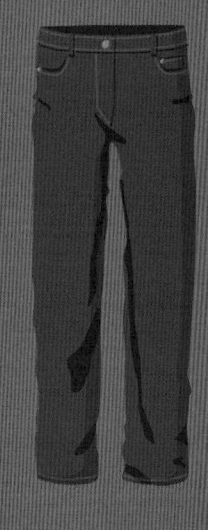

pants
un pantalon
(uh pon-ta-lon)

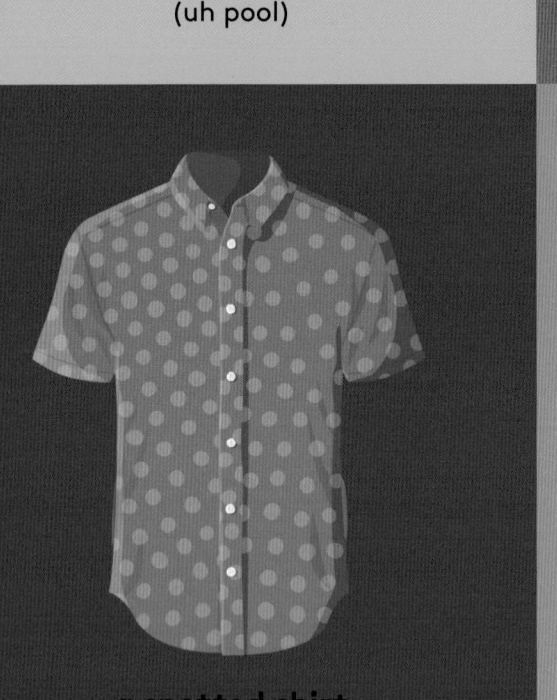

a spotted shirt
une chemise à pois
(oon shuh-meez a pwah)

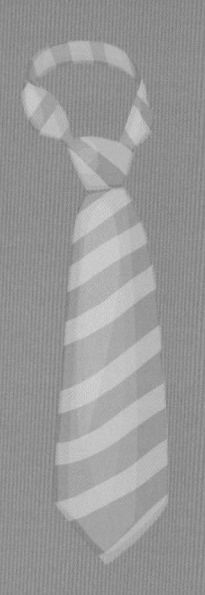

a striped tie
une cravate à rayures
(oon kra-vat a ray-uhr)

What is she wearing?
Qu'est-ce qu'elle porte?
(kes kel port)

She is wearing …
Elle porte …
(el port)

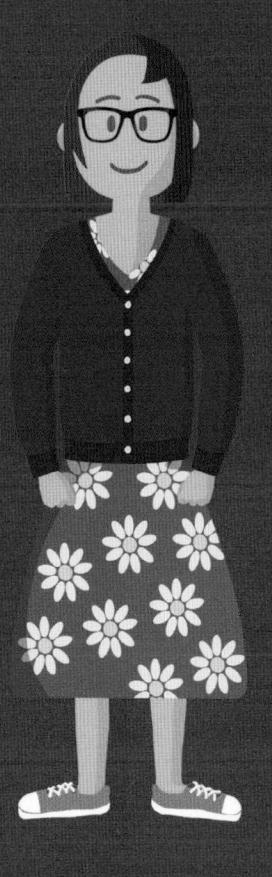

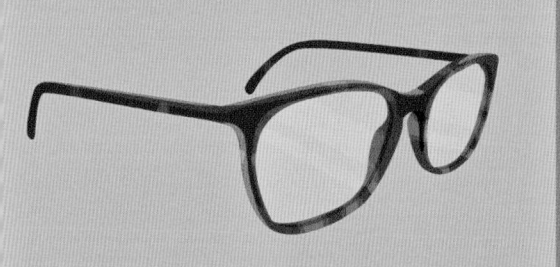

glasses
des lunettes

(day loo-net)

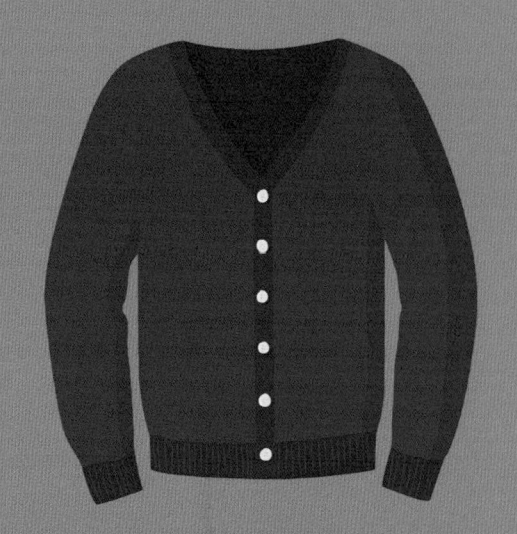

a cardigan
un cardigan

(uh kar-dee-goh)

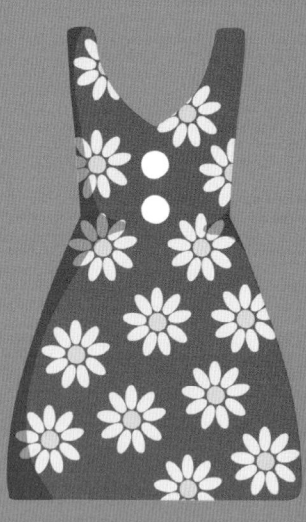

a pretty dress
une jolie robe

(oon jho-lee rob)

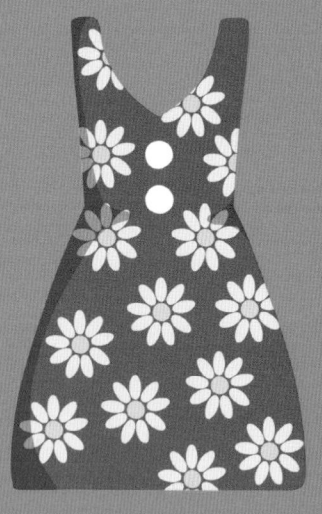

gray sneakers
des baskets grises

(day bas-ket greez)

79

My T-shirt is ...
Mon tee-shirt est ...
(mon tee-shert eh)

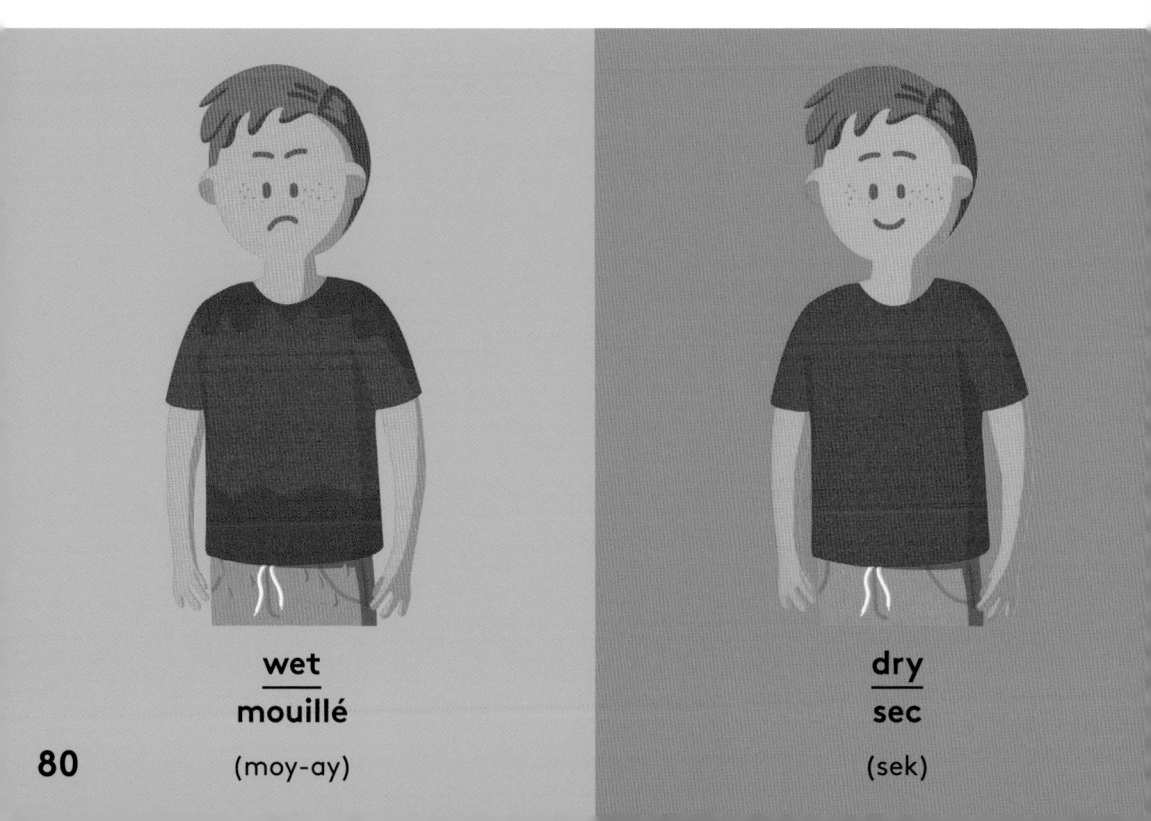

wet
mouillé
(moy-ay)

dry
sec
(sek)

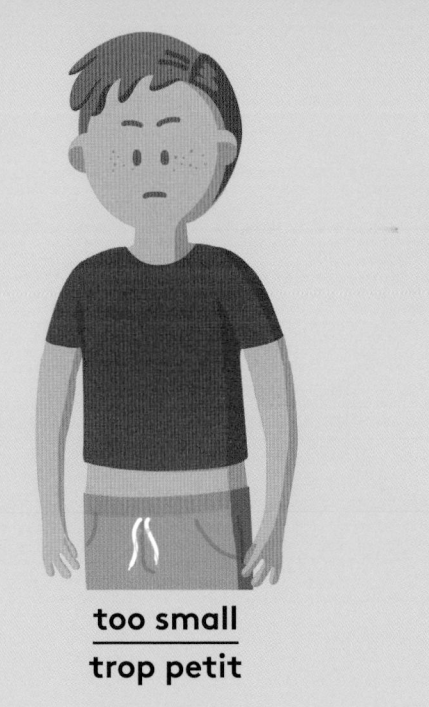

too small
trop petit

(troh ptee)

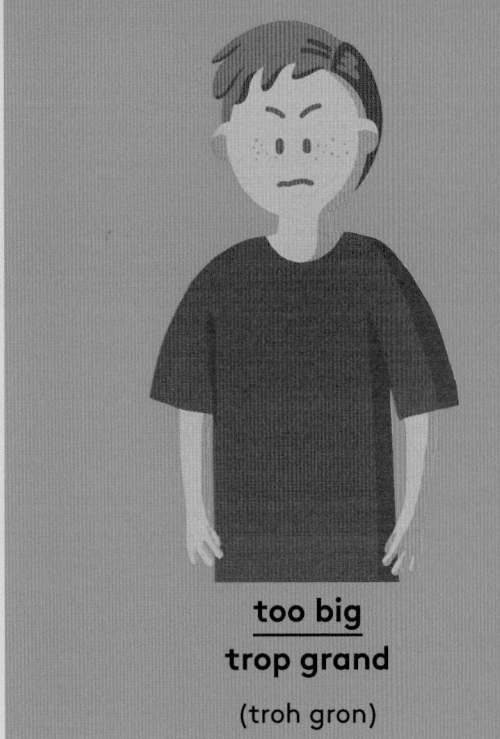

too big
trop grand

(troh gron)

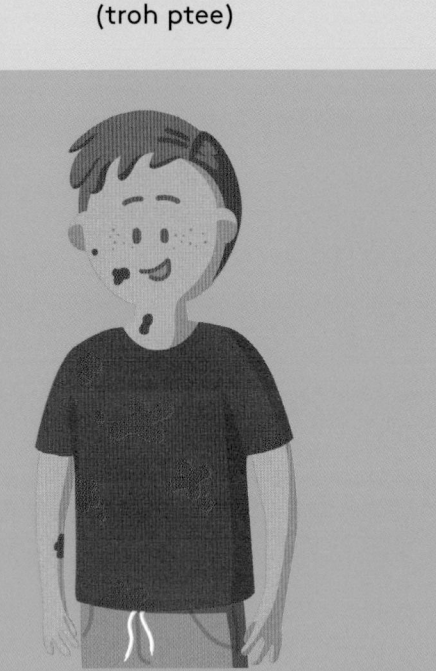

dirty
sale

(sal)

torn
déchiré

(deh-sheer-ay)

Do you have any pets?
As-tu des animaux chez toi?

(a-too dayz an-ee-moh
shay twah)

I don't have any pets.
Je n'ai pas d'animal.

(jhuh nay pa dan-ee-mal)

Yes, I have two pets.
Oui, j'ai deux animaux chez moi.

(wee jhay duhz an-ee-moh shay mwah)

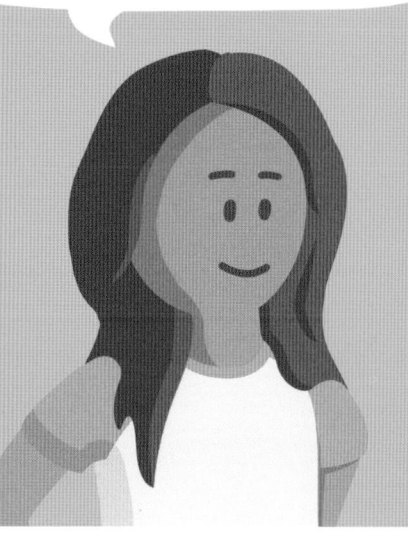
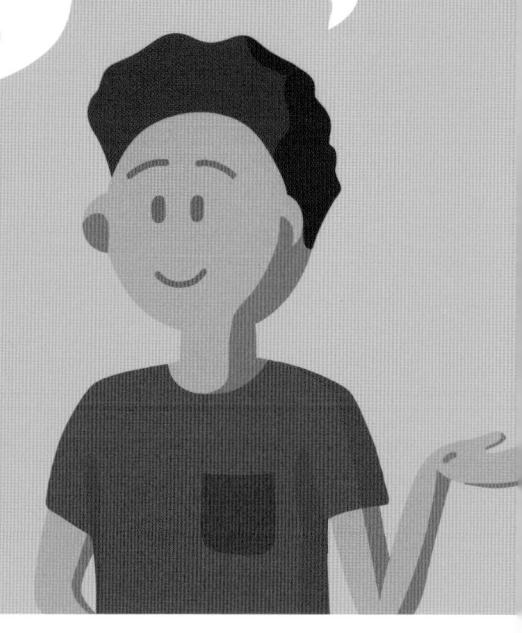

I have ...
J'ai ...
(jhay)

a mouse
une souris

(oon soo-ree)

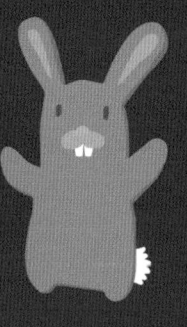

a rabbit
un lapin

(uh la-pa)

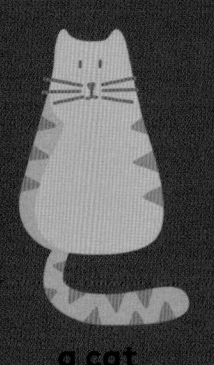

a cat
un chat

(uh sha)

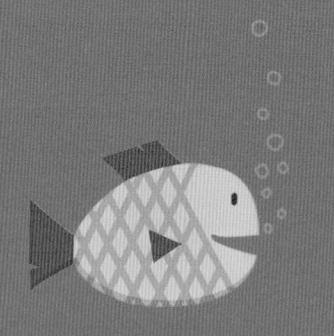

a horse
un cheval

(uh shuh-val)

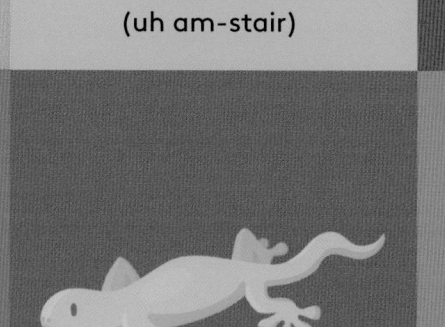

a hamster
un hamster

(uh am-stair)

a dog
un chien

(uh shee-eh)

a fish
un poisson

(uh pwa-son)

a lizard
un lézard

(uh lehz-ahr)

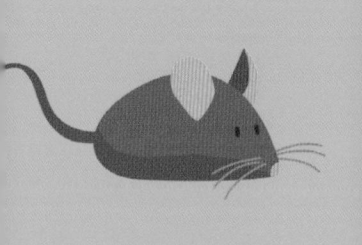

a bird
un oiseau

(uhn wa-zoh)

What's she like?
Elle est comment?

(el eh ko-mon)

What's he like?
Il est comment?

(eel eh ko-mon)

She is playful.
Elle est enjouée.

(el eh on-jhoo-ay)

He is cute.
Il est mignon.

(eel eh meen-yoh)

She is funny.
Elle est drôle.

(el eh drohl)

He is clever.
Il est intelligent.

(eel eh an-tel-ee-jhon)

She is friendly.
Elle est amicale.

(el eh a-mee-kal)

He is crazy.
Il est fou.

(eel eh foo)

84

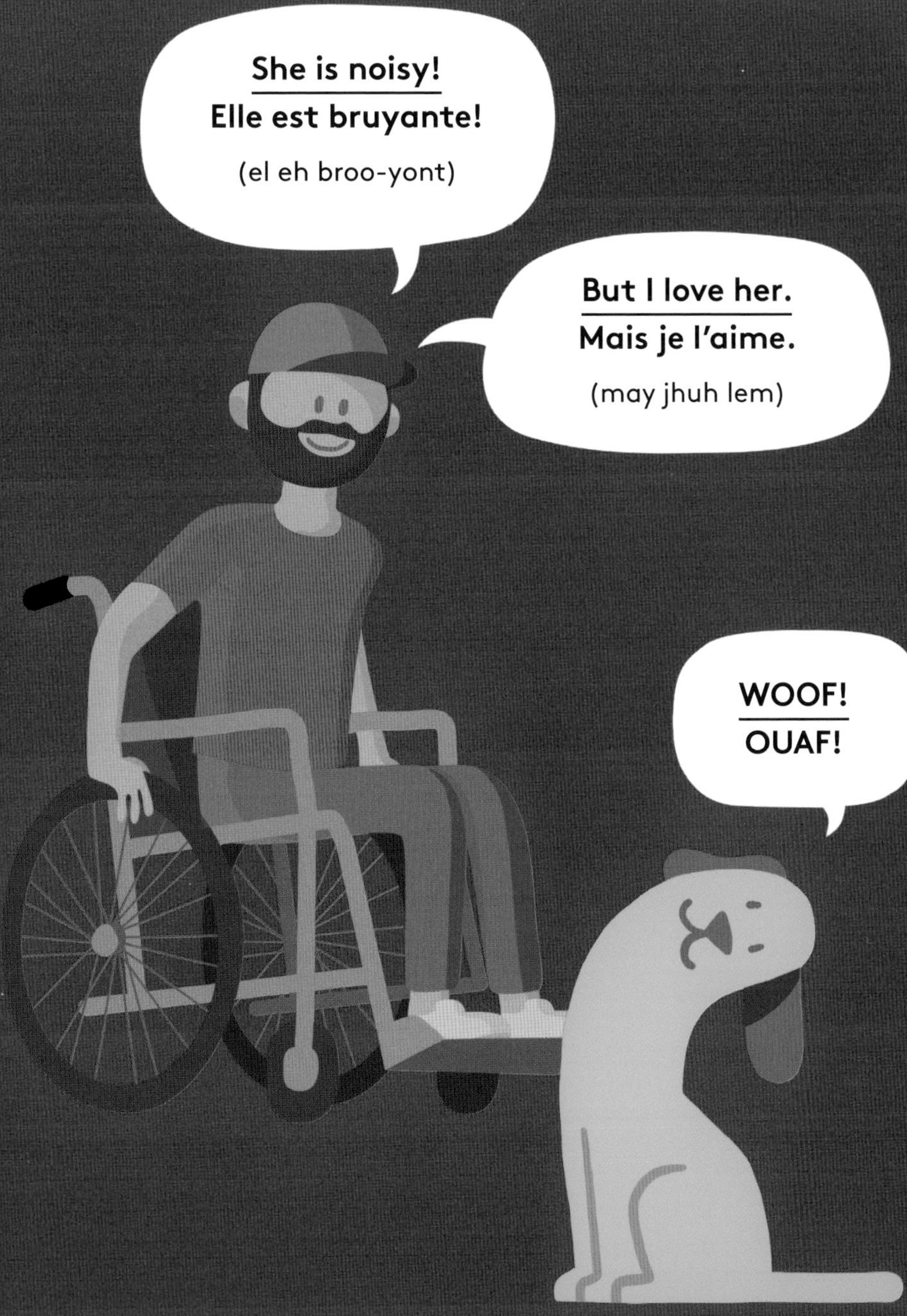
She is noisy!
Elle est bruyante!
(el eh broo-yont)
But I love her.
Mais je l'aime.
(may jhuh lem)
WOOF!
OUAF!

Today it's …
Il fait … aujourd'hui
(eel fay … oh-jhoor-dwee)

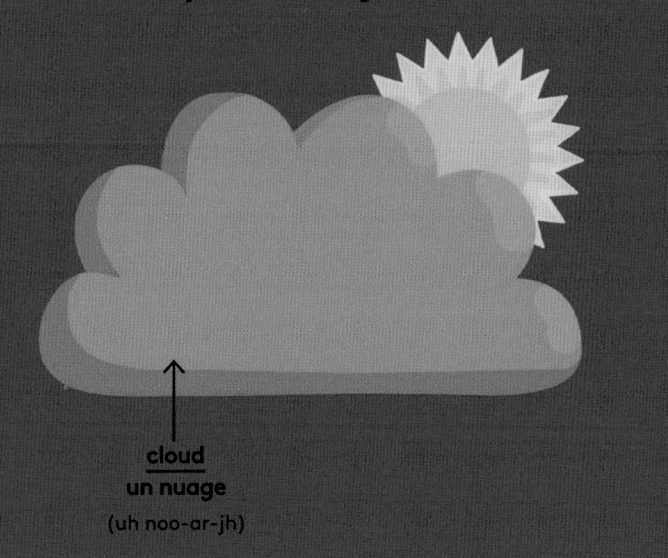

cloud
un nuage
(uh noo-ar-jh)

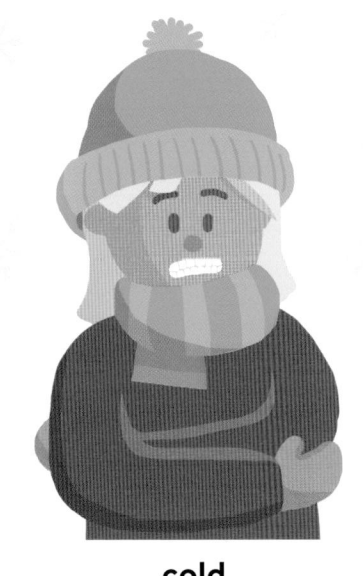

hot
chaud

(show)

cold
froid

(frwah)

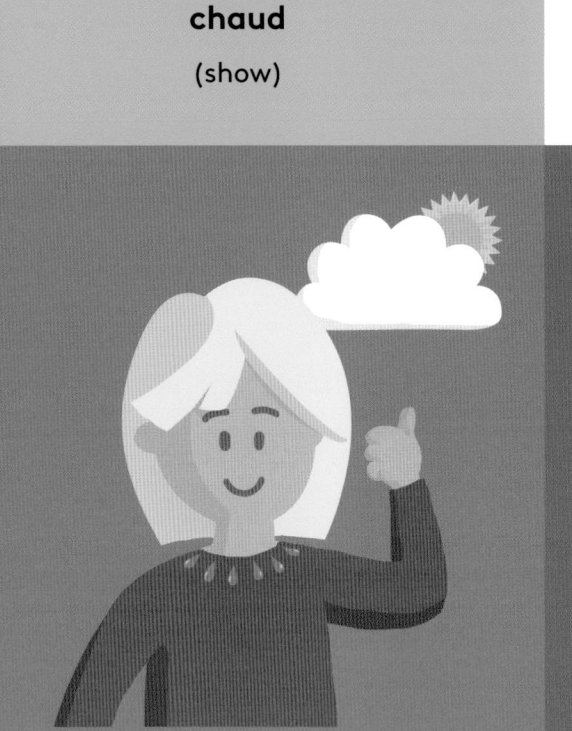

fine
beau

(boh)

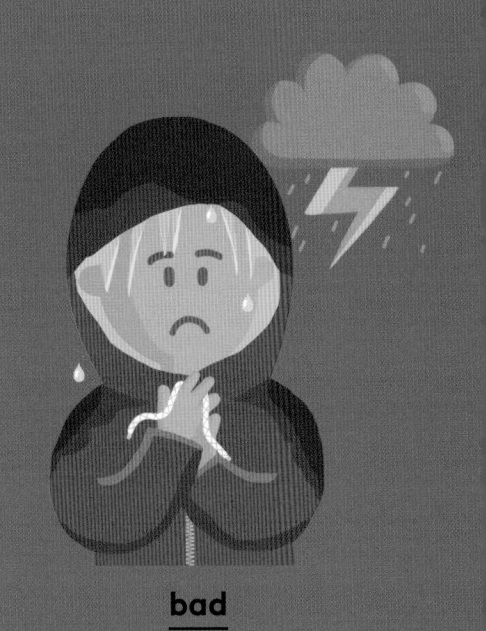

bad
mauvais

(moh-vay)

**What will the weather
be tomorrow?**
Quel temps fera-t-il demain?
(kel tahn fuh-ra-teel duh-ma)

Tomorrow it will be ...
Demain il y aura ...
(duh-ma eel yor-ah)

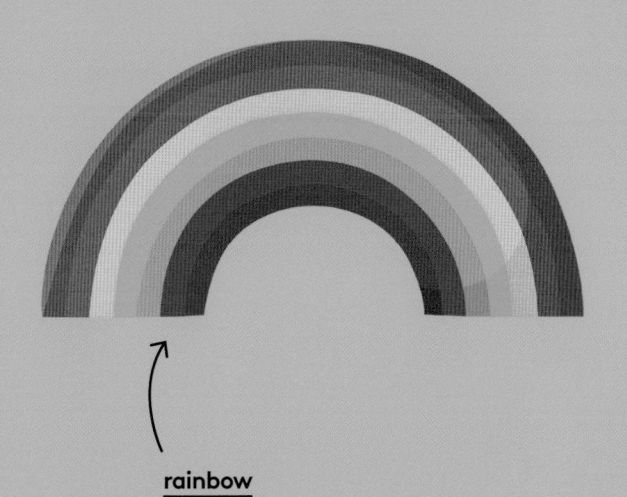

rainbow
un arc-en-ciel
(uhn ark-on-see-yay)

windy
du vent

(doo von)

stormy
un orage

(uhn or-ar-jh)

cloudy
des nuages

(day noo-ar-jh)

foggy
du brouillard

(doo broo-yar)

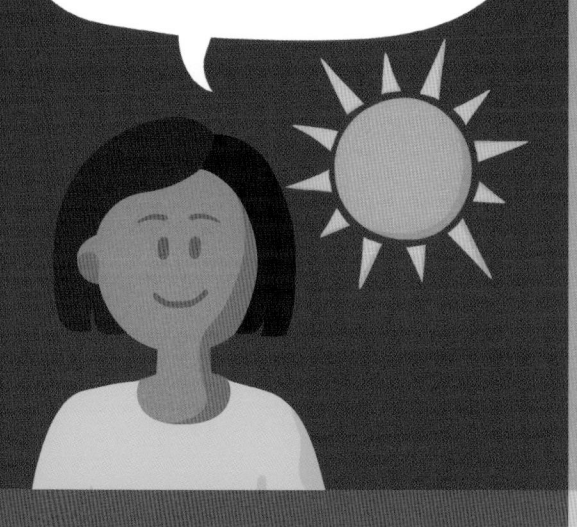

It's sunny! I will wear ...
Il y a du soleil! Je vais porter ...

(eel ya doo soh-lay
jhuh vay por-tay)

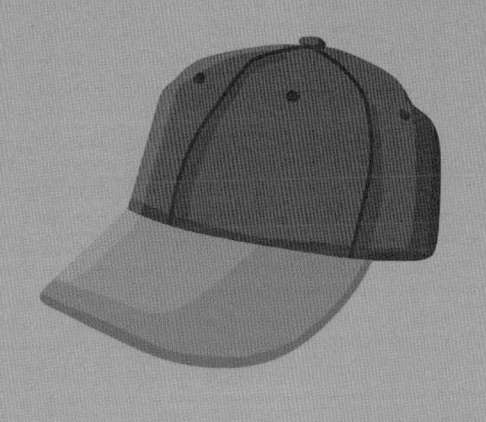

my cap
ma casquette

(ma kass-ket)

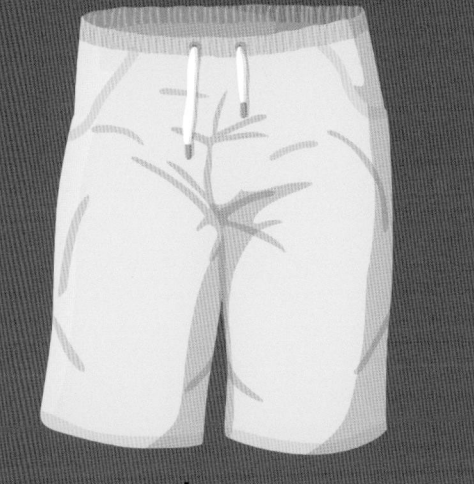

shorts
un short

(uh shor)

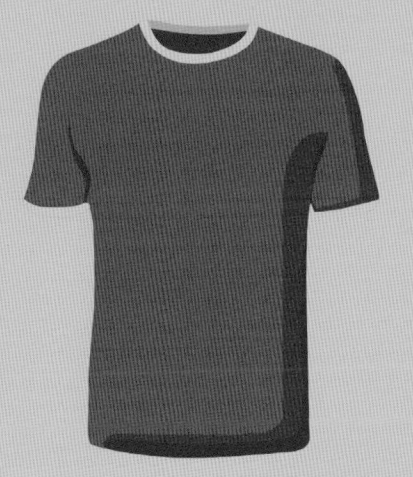

a T-shirt
un tee-shirt

(uh tee-shert)

It's raining! I need …

Il pleut! J'ai besoin de …

(eel pluh jhay buh-zwan duh)

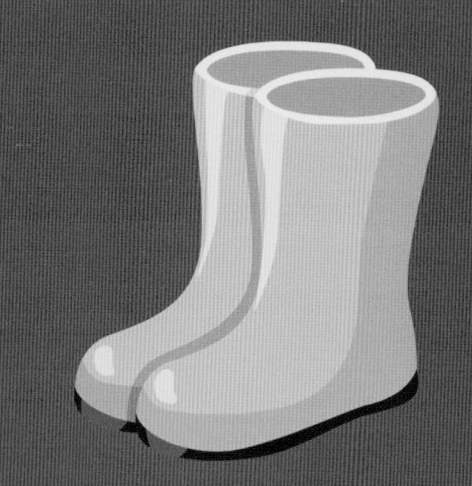

my umbrella

mon parapluie

(mon pa-ra-plwee)

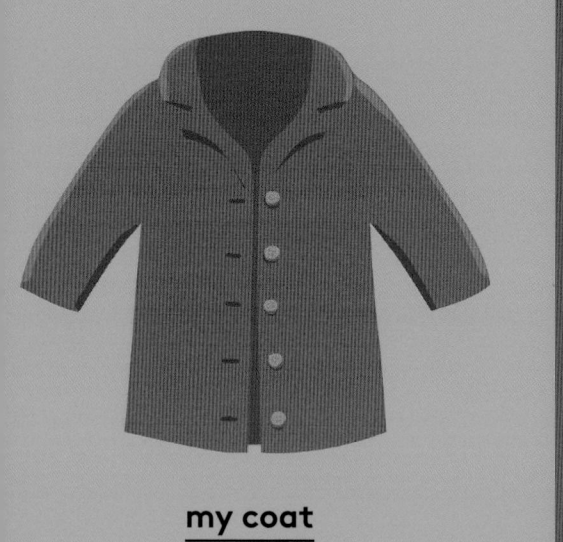

my coat

mon manteau

(mon man-toh)

my boots

mes bottes

(may bot)

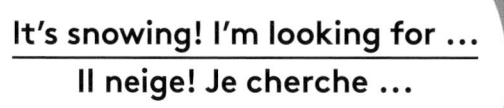

It's snowing! I'm looking for ...
Il neige! Je cherche ...

(eel neh-jh jhuh shair-sh)

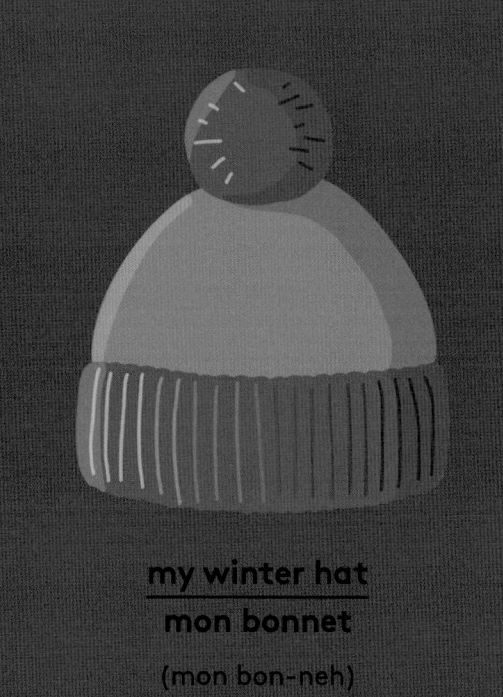

my winter hat
mon bonnet

(mon bon-neh)

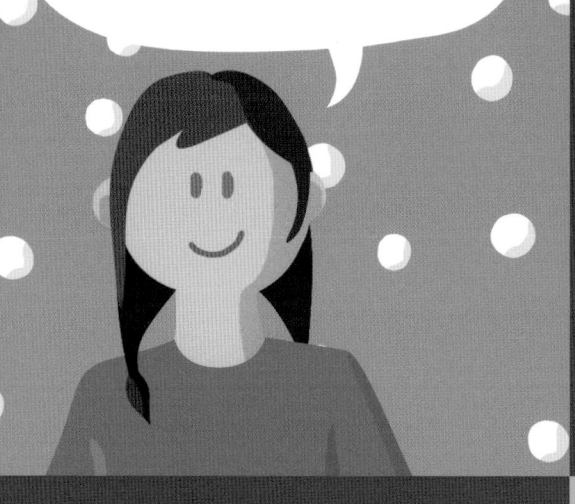

my scarf
mon écharpe

(mon eh-sharp)

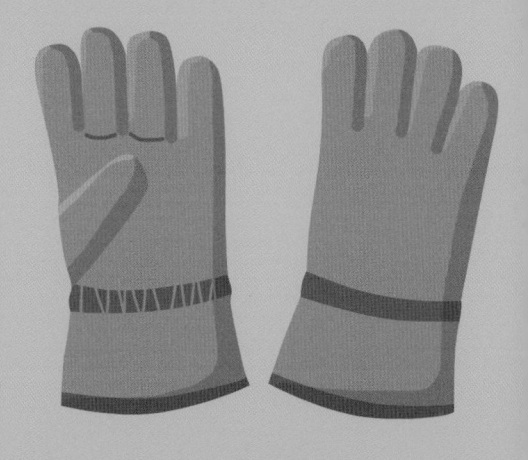

my gloves
mes gants

(may gon)

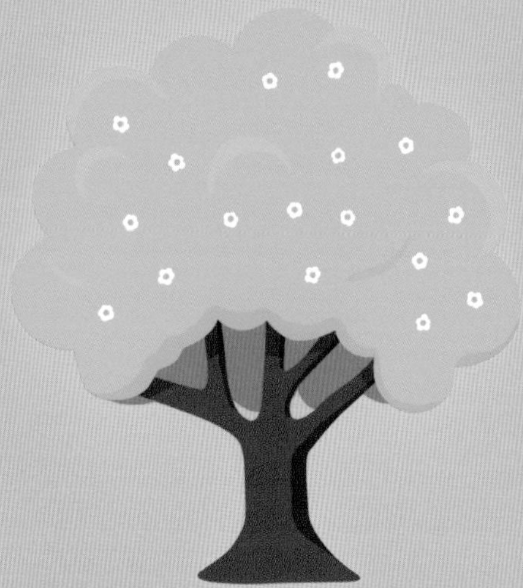

spring
le printemps

(luh pra-toh)

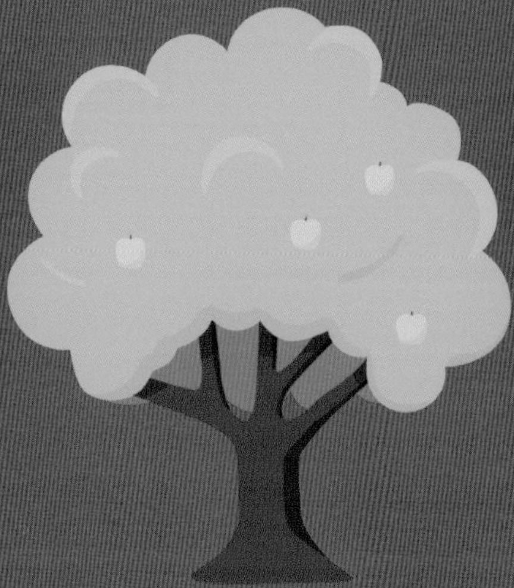

summer
l'été

(let-ay)

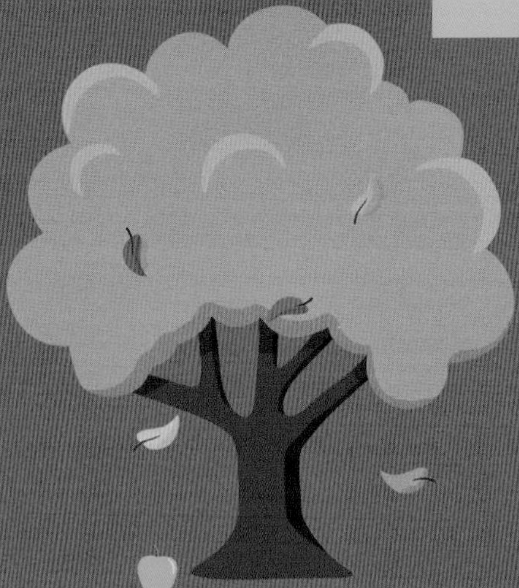

The seasons
Les saisons

(lay say-zon)

fall
l'automne

(low-ton)

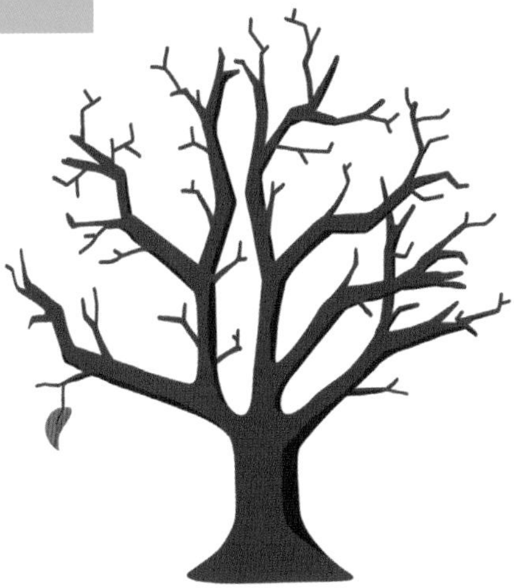

winter
l'hiver

(lee-vair)

Are you OK?
Ça va?
(sa va)

Remember, in French,
adjectives change
depending on the noun.
In this case, the noun is
yourself, so the adjectives
change depending on
whether you are male
or female.

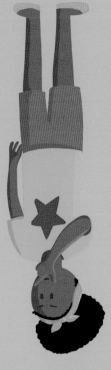

I feel ...
Je me sens ...
(jhuh muh sonz)

How do you feel?
Comment ça va?
(Ko-mon sa va)

nervous
nerveux (m) / nerveuse (f)
(nair-vuh / nair-vuhz)

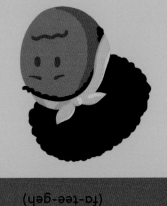

angry
fâché (m) / fâchée (f)
(fash-ay)

tired
fatigué (m) / fatiguée (f)
(fa-tee-geh)

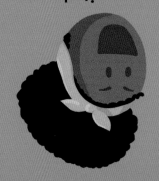

excited
impatient (m) / impatiente (f)
(am-pas-ee-on / am-pas-ee-ont)

happy
heureux (m) / heureuse (f)
(er-er / er-erz)

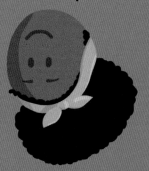

sad
triste
(treest)

I have a cough.
Je tousse.
(jhuh too-ss)

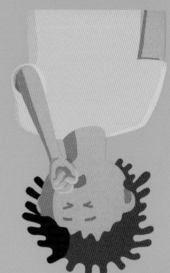

I have a cold.
J'ai un rhume.
(jhay uh room)

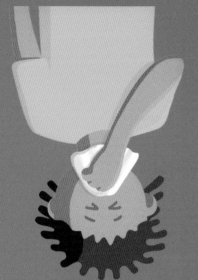

I don't feel well!
Je me sens mal!
(jhuh muh sonz mal)

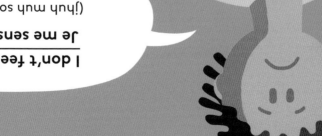

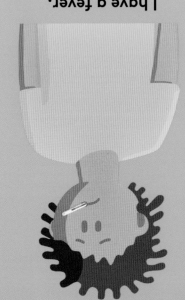

I have a fever.
J'ai une fièvre.
(jhay oon fee-air-vruh)

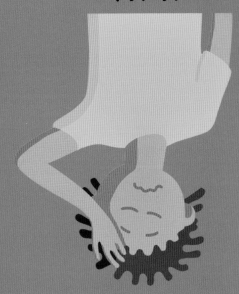

I feel faint.
Je me sens faible.
(jhuh sonz fay-bluh)

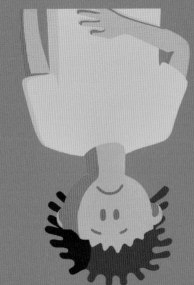

I have a stomachache.
J'ai mal au ventre.
(jhay mal oh von-truh)

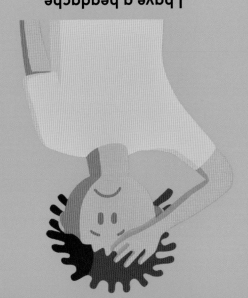

I have a headache.
J'ai mal à la tête.
(jhay mal a la tet)

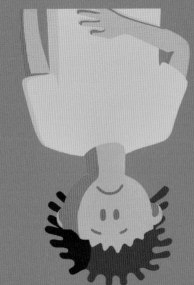

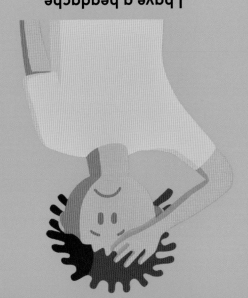

Where does it hurt?
Où est-ce que tu as mal?

(oo es kuh too a mal)

My ... hurts
J'ai mal ...
(jhay mal)

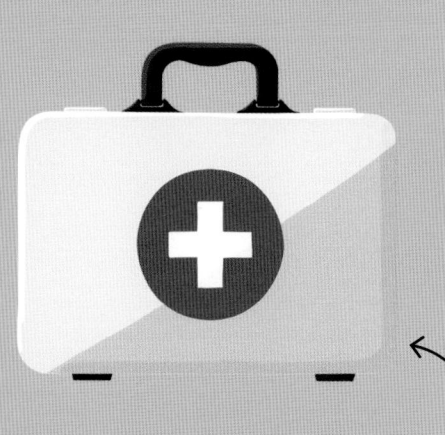

first aid kit
une trousse de premier secours
(oon trooss duh prem-ee-air suh-kor)

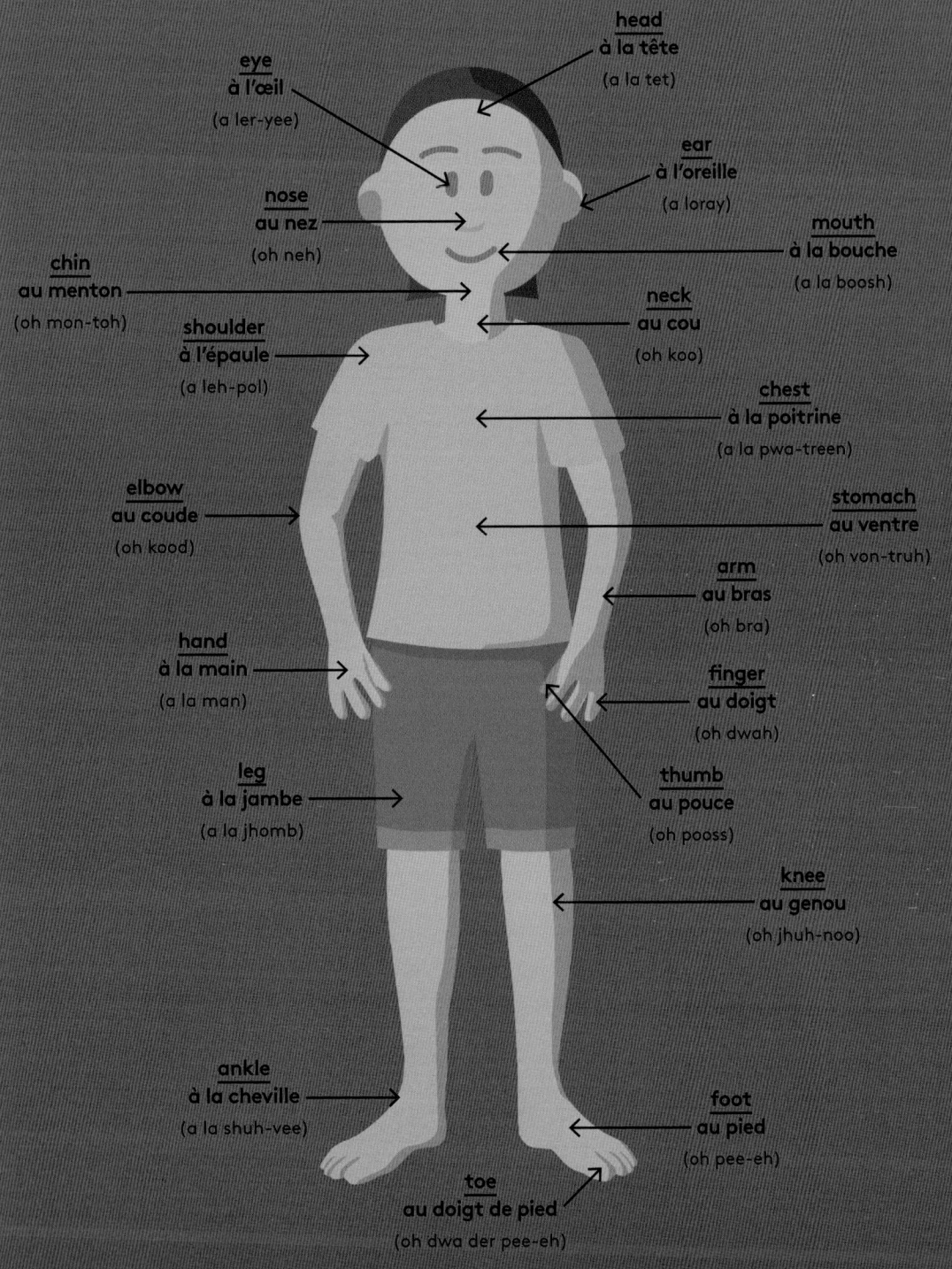

head
à la tête
(a la tet)

eye
à l'œil
(a ler-yee)

ear
à l'oreille
(a loray)

nose
au nez
(oh neh)

mouth
à la bouche
(a la boosh)

chin
au menton
(oh mon-toh)

neck
au cou
(oh koo)

shoulder
à l'épaule
(a leh-pol)

chest
à la poitrine
(a la pwa-treen)

elbow
au coude
(oh kood)

stomach
au ventre
(oh von-truh)

arm
au bras
(oh bra)

hand
à la main
(a la man)

finger
au doigt
(oh dwah)

leg
à la jambe
(a la jhomb)

thumb
au pouce
(oh pooss)

knee
au genou
(oh jhuh-noo)

ankle
à la cheville
(a la shuh-vee)

foot
au pied
(oh pee-eh)

toe
au doigt de pied
(oh dwa der pee-eh)

99

You need some medicine.
Tu as besoin d'un médicament.

(too a buh-zwan duh meh-dee-ka-moh)

medicine
le médicament

(luh med-ee-ka-moh)

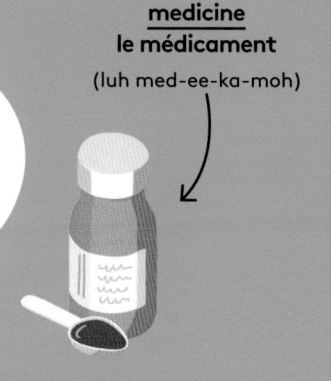

Go to ...
Allez ...
(a-lay)

Get well soon!
Bon rétablissement!

(bon reh-tab-lees-moh)

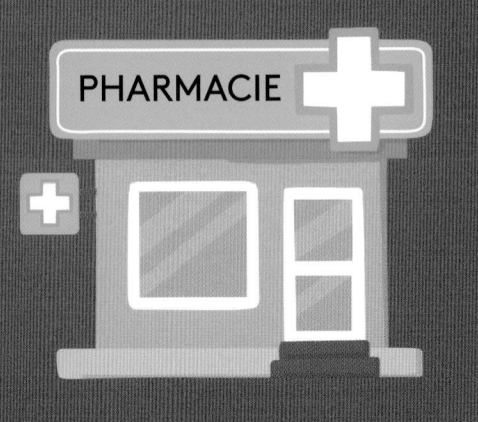

the pharmacy
à la pharmacie

(a la far-ma-see)

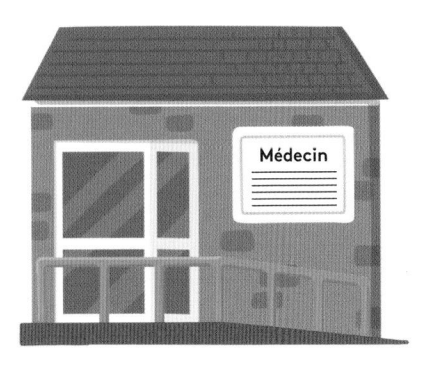

the doctor's office
chez le médecin

(shay luh med-san)

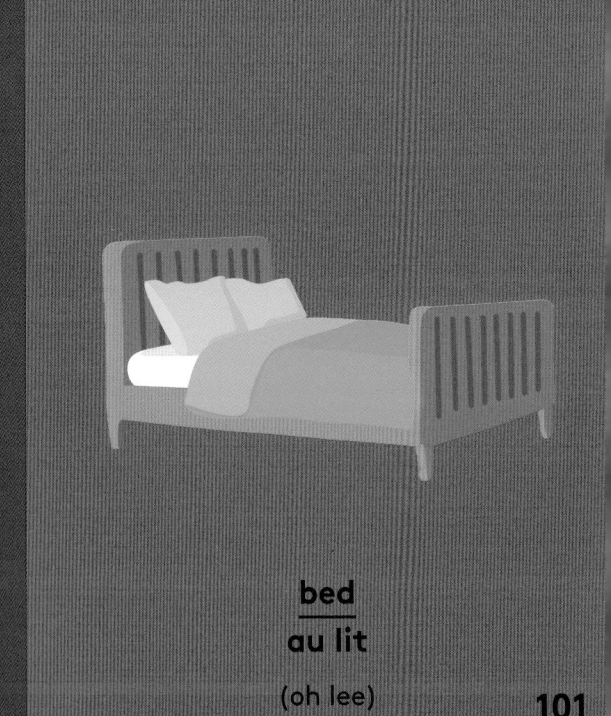

the hospital
à l'hôpital

(a lo-pee-tal)

bed
au lit

(oh lee)

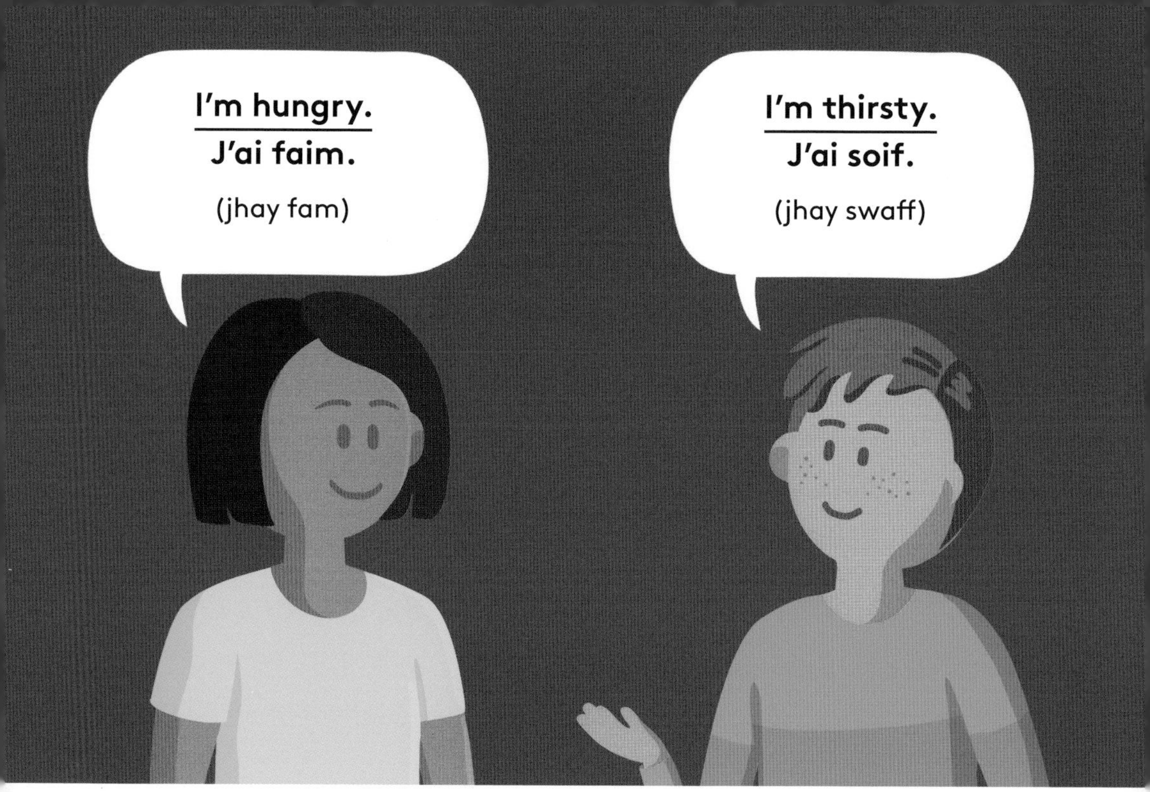
I'm hungry.
J'ai faim.
(jhay fam)
I'm thirsty.
J'ai soif.
(jhay swaff)

Let's go to the café for ...

Allons prendre ... au café

(a-lon pron-dr ... oh ka-fay)

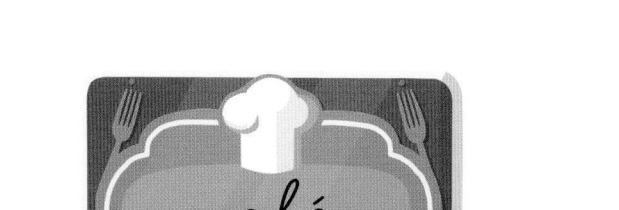

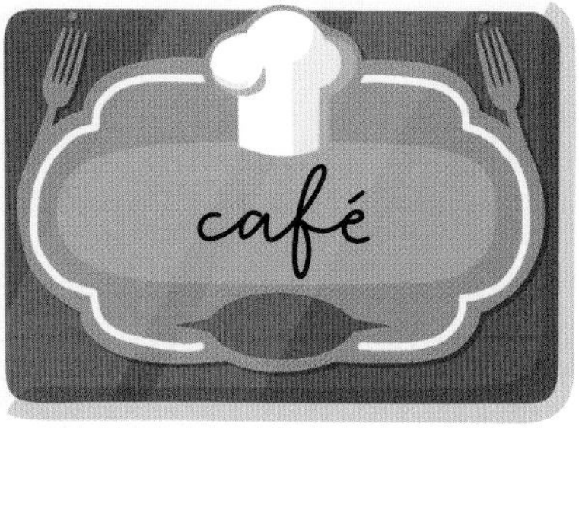
café

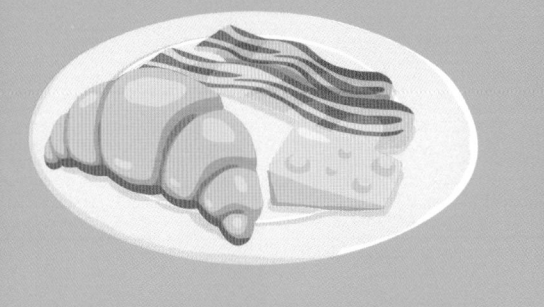

breakfast
le petit déjeuner

(luh ptee deh-jher-neh)

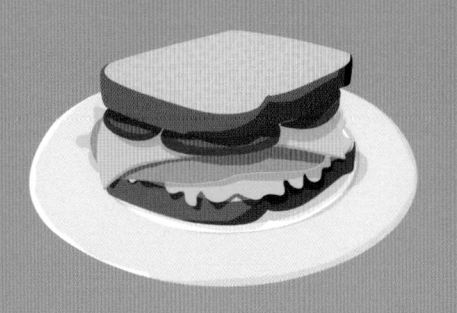

lunch
le déjeuner

(luh deh-jher-neh)

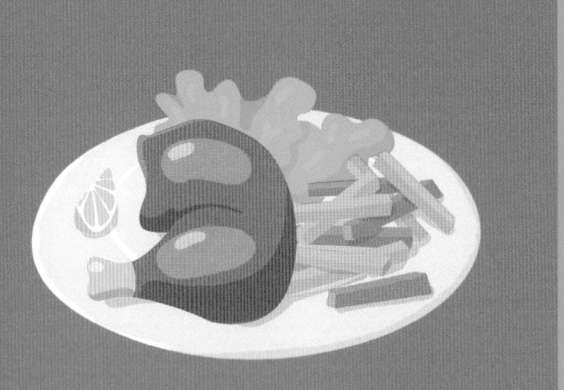

dinner
le dîner

(luh dee-neh)

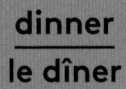

a drink
une boisson

(oon bwa-son)

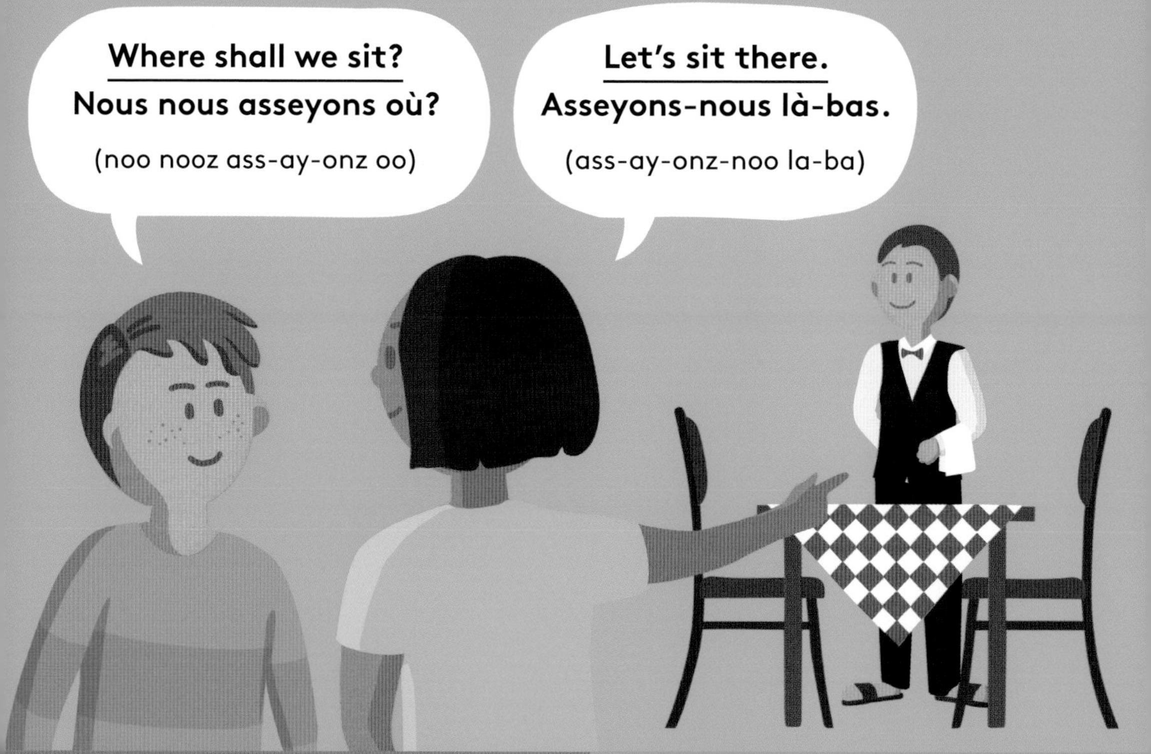

Where shall we sit?
Nous nous asseyons où?
(noo nooz ass-ay-onz oo)

Let's sit there.
Asseyons-nous là-bas.
(ass-ay-onz-noo la-ba)

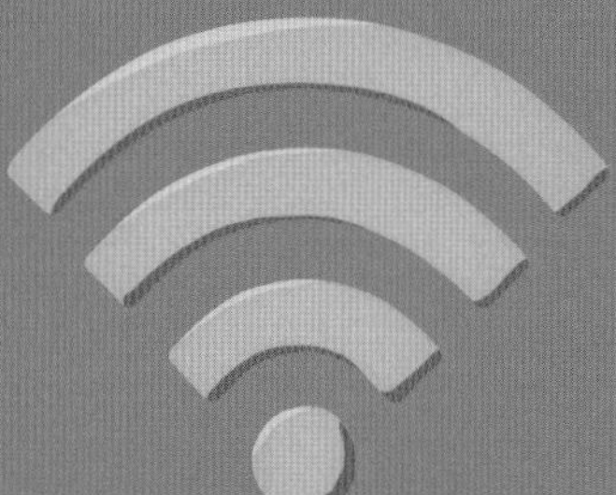

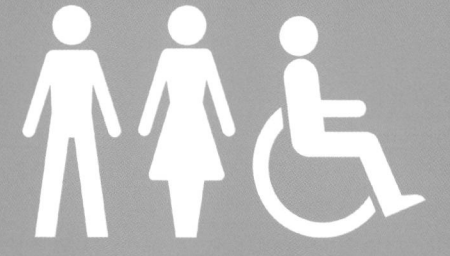

Do you have Wi-Fi?
Avez-vous le WiFi?
(a-vay-voo luh wee-fee)

Do you have a restroom?
Avez-vous des toilettes?
(a-vay-voo day twa-let)

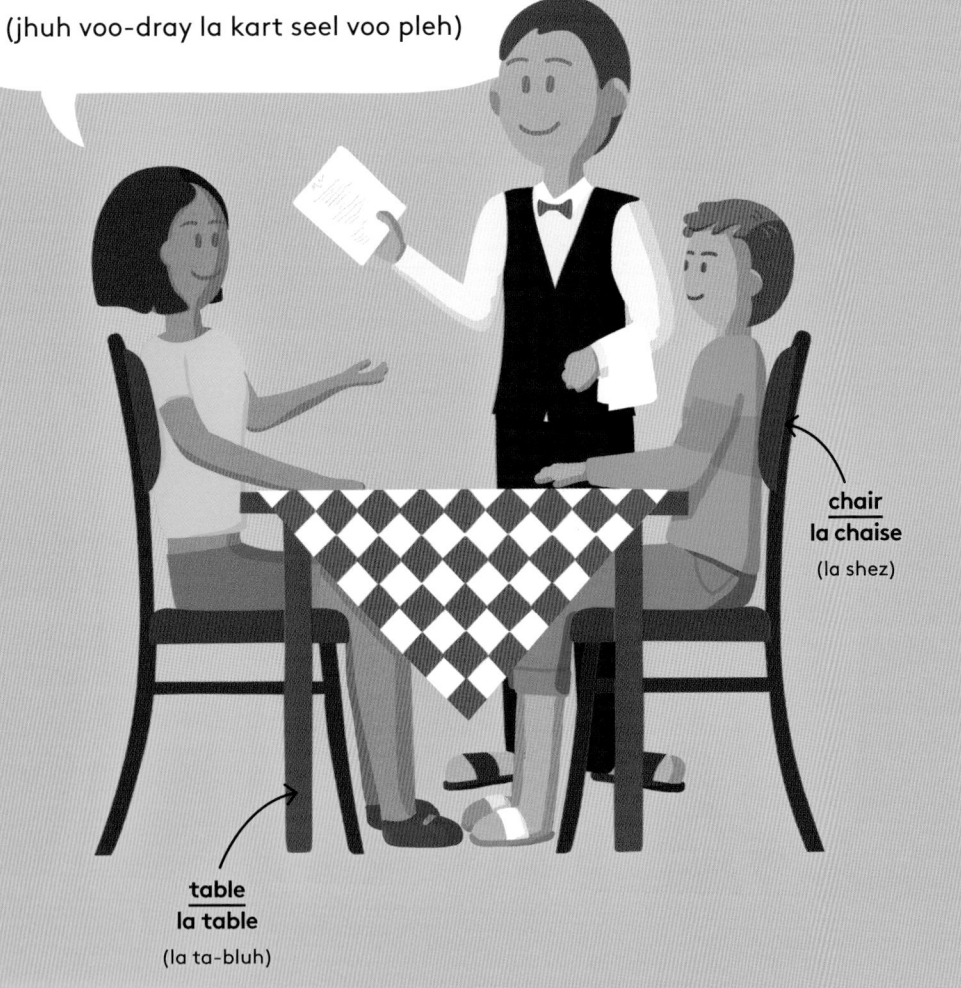

105

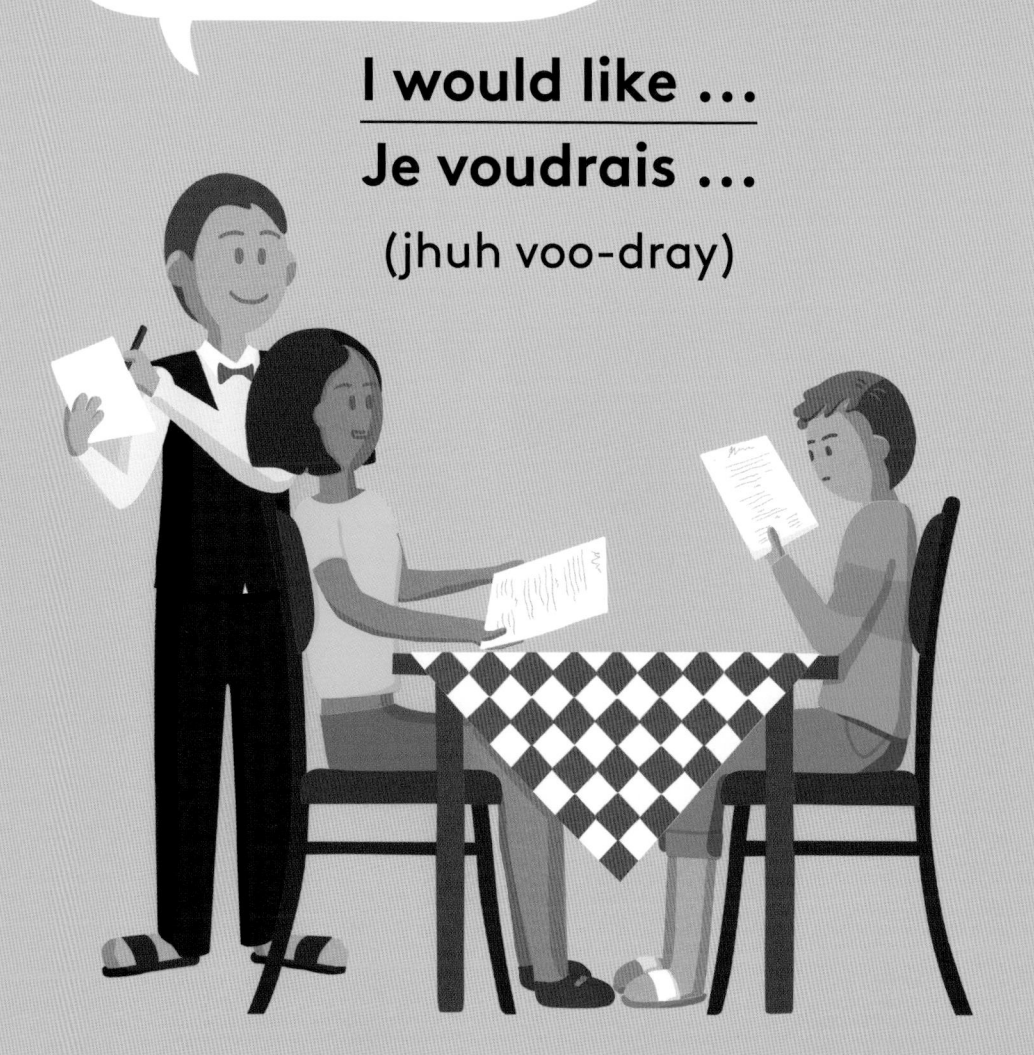

Are you ready to order?
Êtes-vous prêt à commander?
(et-voo pret a kom-on-day)

I would like …
Je voudrais …
(jhuh voo-dray)

an ice cream
une glace

(oon glas)

a sandwich
un sandwich

(uh sond-weech)

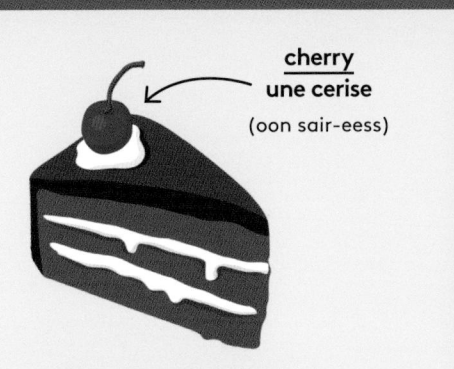

cherry
une cerise

(oon sair-eess)

a piece of cake
une part de gâteau

(oon pahr duh ga-toh)

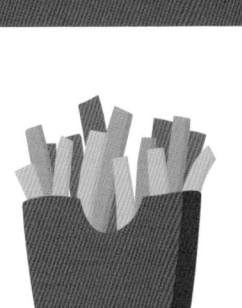

a salad
une salade verte

(oon sa-lad vairt)

a burger
un hamburger

(uhn om-buhr-guhr)

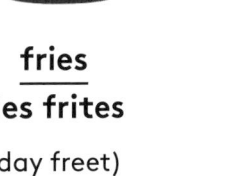

fries
des frites

(day freet)

107

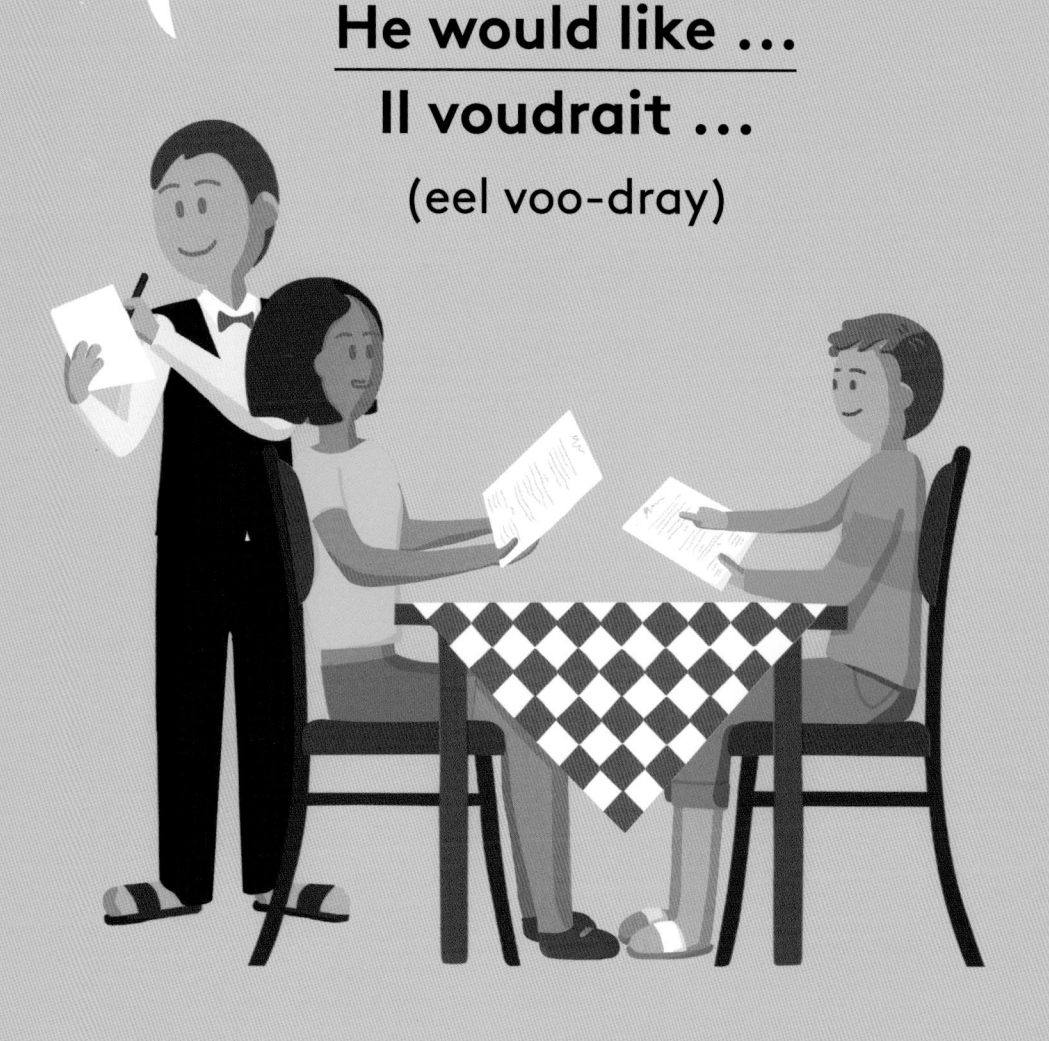

And your friend?
Et votre ami (m)?
(ay vot-r am-ee)

He would like ...
Il voudrait ...
(eel voo-dray)

coffee
un café
(uh kaf-ay)

cola
un coca
(uh koh-ka)

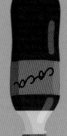

lemonade
une limonade
(oon lee-mon-ad)

orange juice
un jus d'orange
(uh jhoo dor-an-jh)

apple juice
un jus de pomme
(uh jhoo duh pom)

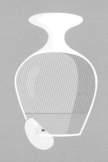

water
de l'eau
(duh loh)

strawberry
la fraise
(la frez)

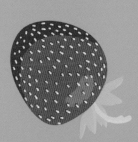

vanilla
la vanille
(la van-ee)

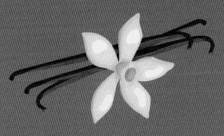

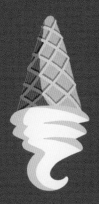

My favorite flavor is ...
Mon parfum préféré est ...
(mon par-fa pref-air-ay eh)

What's your favorite flavor?
Quel parfum préfères-tu?
(kel par-fa pref-air-too)

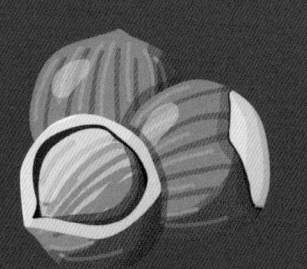

hazelnut
la noisette

(la nwa-zet)

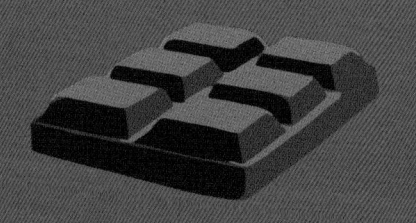

chocolate
le chocolat

(luh sho-koh-la)

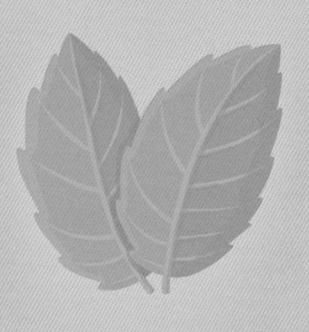

mint
la menthe

(la mont)

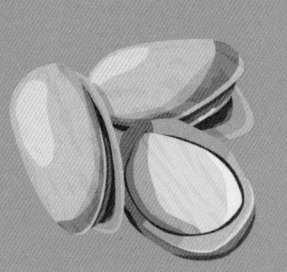

pistachio
la pistache

(la pee-stash)

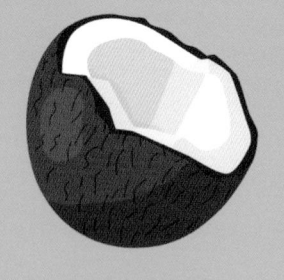

coconut
la noix de coco

(la nwa duh koh-koh)

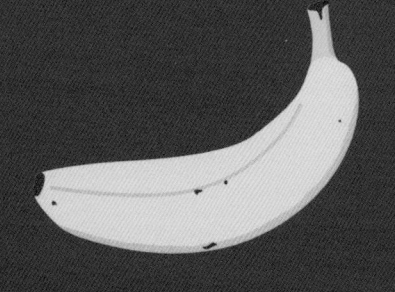

banana
la banane

(la ba-nan)

I don't like tomatoes either.
Je n'aime pas les tomates non plus.
(jhuh nem pa lay toh-mat non ploo)

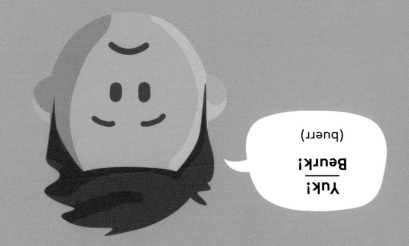

Yuk!
Beurk!
(buerr)

I don't like ...
Je n'aime pas ...
(jhuh nem pa)

pasta
les pâtes
(lay pat)

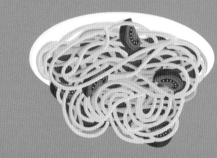

pizza
la pizza
(la peet-za)

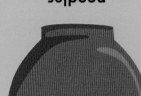

chicken
le poulet
(luh poo-lay)

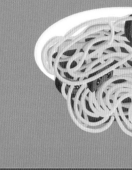

noodles
les nouilles
(lay noo-wee)

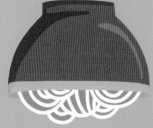

tomatoes
les tomates
(lay toh-mat)

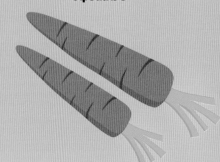

carrots
les carottes
(lay ka-rot)

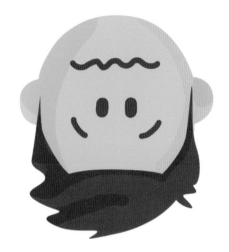

I'm allergic to ...

Je suis allergique ...

(jhuh swee al-air-jheek)

wheat
au blé
(oh blay)

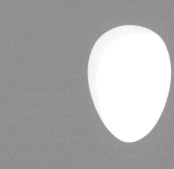

eggs
aux œufs
(oh zuhf)

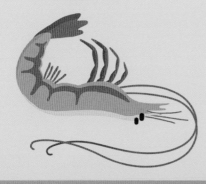

shellfish
aux fruits de mer
(oh fwee duh mair)

fish
au poisson
(oh pwa-son)

milk
au lait
(oh lay)

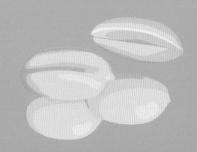

nuts
aux noix
(oh nwah)

a plate
une assiette
(oon ass-ee-et)

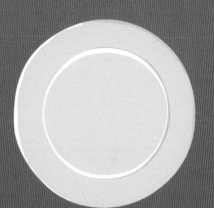

a bowl
un bol
(uh bol)

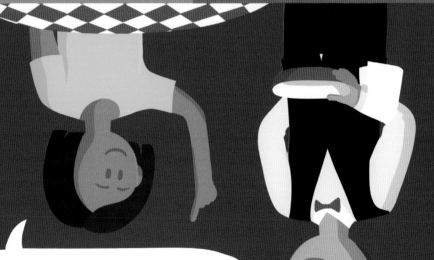

Excuse me. I need …
Excusez-moi. J'ai besoin d' …
(ek-skew-zay-mwah jhay buh-zwan d')

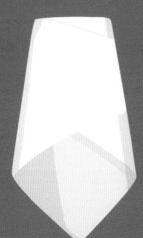

a spoon
une cuillère
(oon kwee-air)

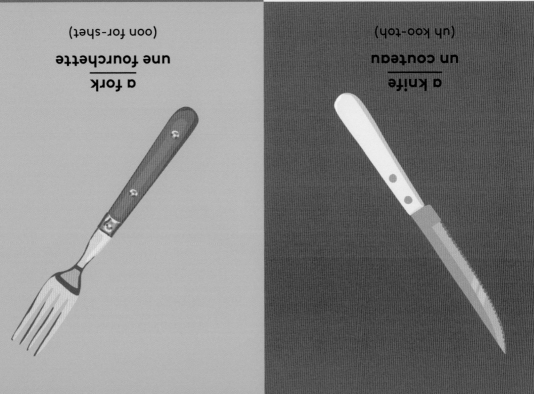

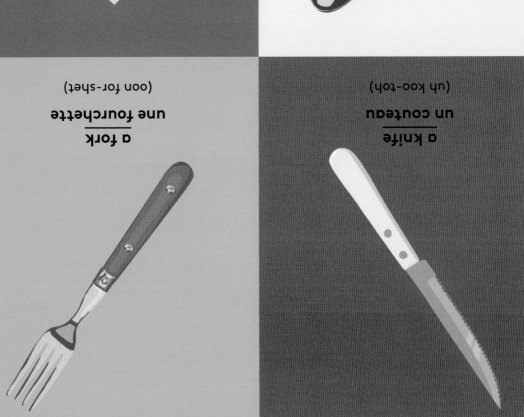

a napkin
une serviette
(oon sair-vee-et)

a fork
une fourchette
(oon for-shet)

a knife
un couteau
(uh koo-toh)

This is delicious!
C'est délicieux!

(seh day-lee-see-uh)

Would you like some more?
En voulez-vous encore?

(on voo-lay-voo on-kor)

I don't like this!
Je n'aime pas ça!

(jhuh nem pa sa)

It's horrible!
C'est dégoûtant!

(seh day-goo-tont)

I can't eat it.
Je ne peux pas le manger.

(jhuh nuh puh pa
luh mon-jhay)

Could I order something else?
Est-ce que je peux commander
autre chose?

(es kuh jhuh puh kom-on-day
oh-tr showz)

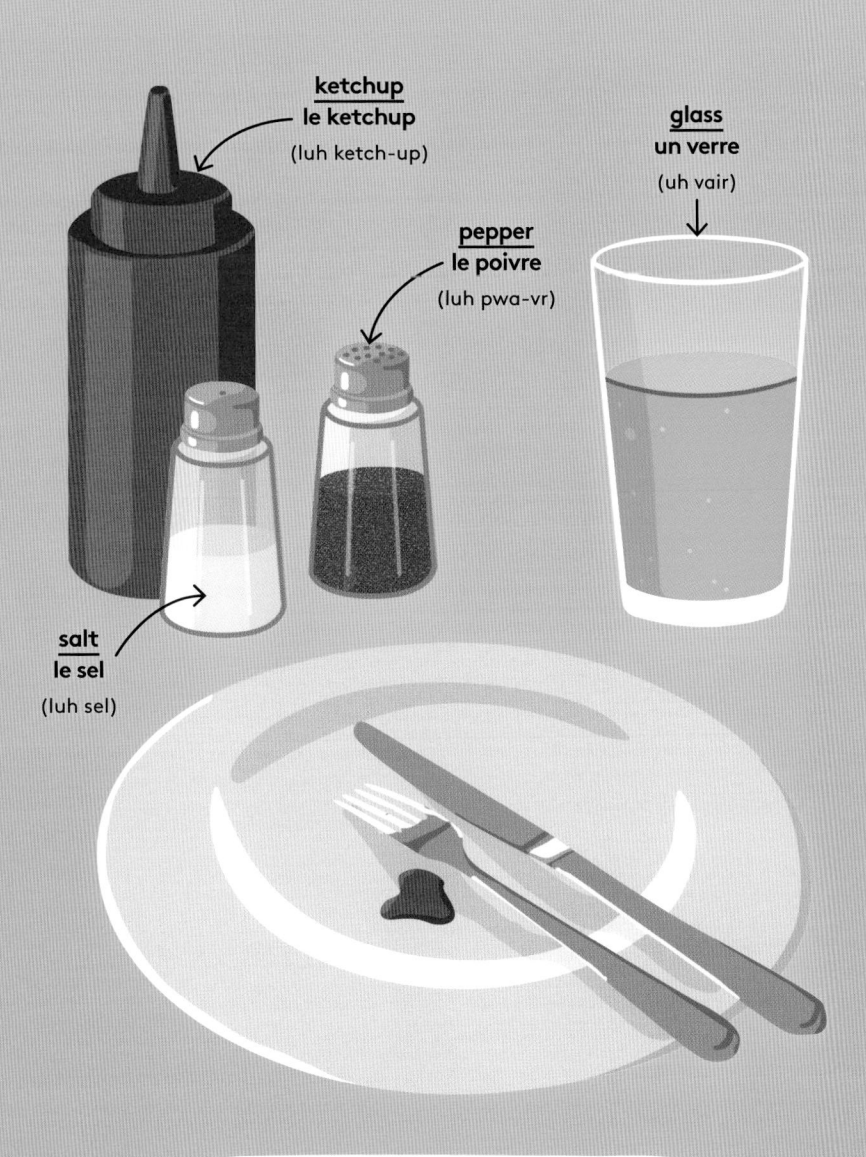

ketchup
le ketchup
(luh ketch-up)

pepper
le poivre
(luh pwa-vr)

glass
un verre
(uh vair)

salt
le sel
(luh sel)

Please can we have the check?
L'addition, s'il vous plaît.

(la-dee-see-on seel voo pleh)

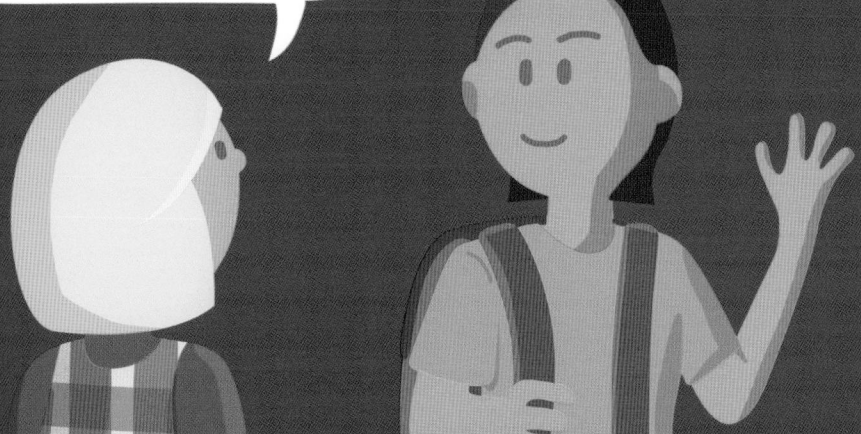

Where are you going?
Où vas-tu?
(oo va-too)

I'm going to school.
Je vais à l'école.
(jhuh vay a leh-kol)

Do you like school?
Aimes-tu l'école?
(em-too leh-kol)

Yes, it's good.
Oui, c'est bien.
(wee seh bee-an)

I like school.
J'aime l'école.
(jhem leh-kol)

No, I don't like school!
Non, je n'aime pas l'école!
(non jhuh nem pa leh-kol)

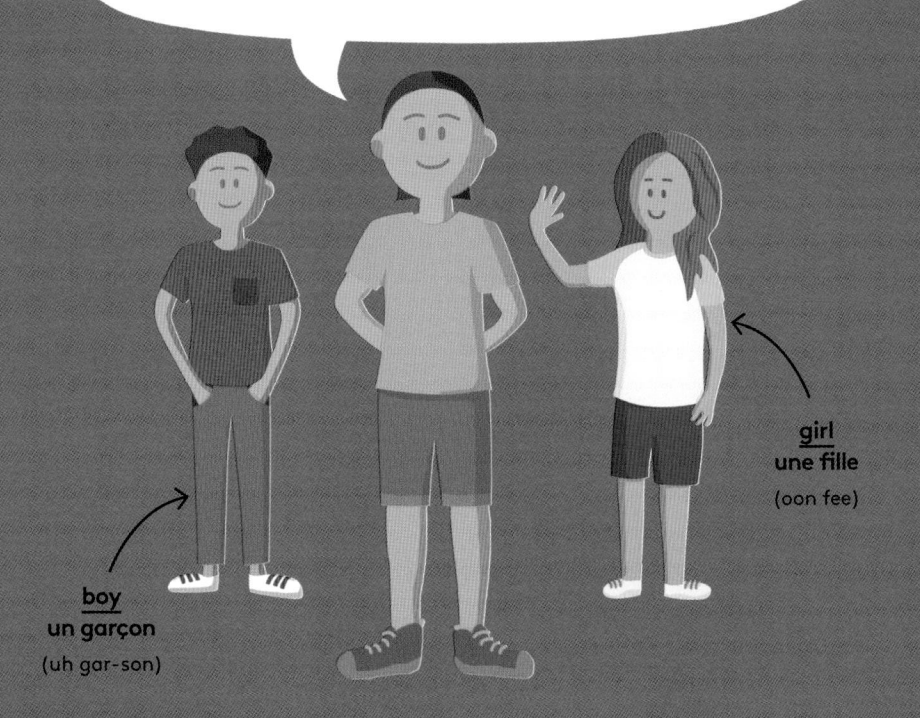

I like school because I see my friends.
J'aime l'école parce que je vois mes amis.

(jhem leh-kol par-se kuh jhuh vwa mayz am-ee)

boy
un garçon
(uh gar-son)

girl
une fille
(oon fee)

My best friend is called ...
Mon meilleur ami s'appelle ...

(mon may-uhr am-ee sa-pel)

If your best friend is female, you would say "**Ma meilleure amie s'appelle ...**"

121

How do you get to school?
Comment vas-tu à l'école?

(ko-mon va-too a leh-kol)

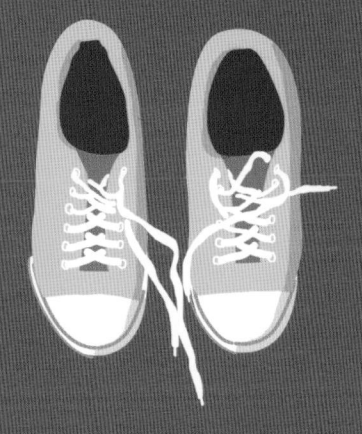

I walk.
Je vais à pied.

(jhuh vay a pee-eh)

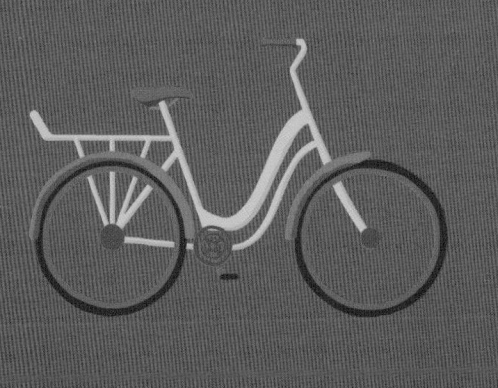

I cycle.
Je vais en vélo.

(jhuh vay on vay-loh)

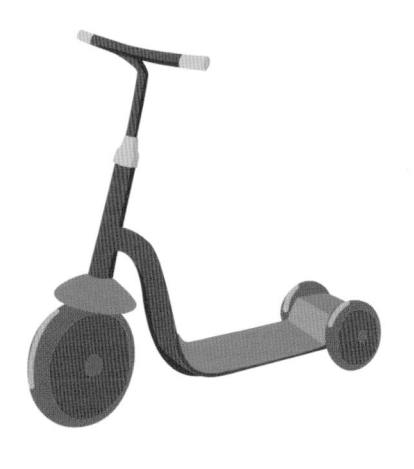

I go by scooter.
Je vais en trottinette.

(jhuh vay on trot-in-et)

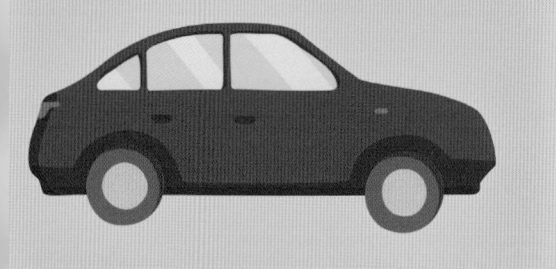

I go in the car.
Je vais en voiture.

(jhuh vay on vwa-tewr)

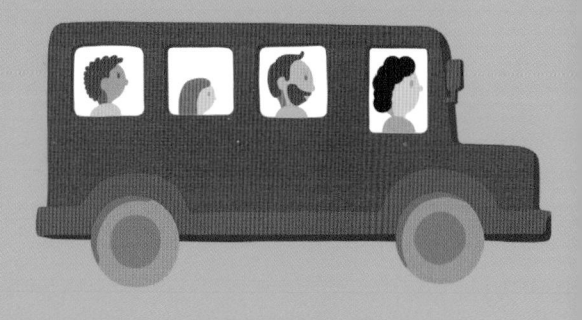

I catch a bus.
Je prends le bus.

(jhuh prond luh boos)

I take the train.
Je prends le train.

(jhuh prond luh tra)

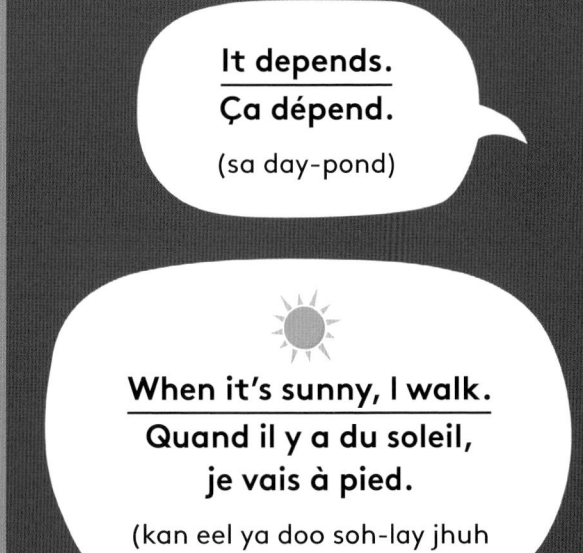

It depends.
Ça dépend.

(sa day-pond)

When it's sunny, I walk.
Quand il y a du soleil,
je vais à pied.

(kan eel ya doo soh-lay jhuh
vay a pee-ay)

What's your favorite subject?
Quelle est ta matière préférée?

(kel eh ta mat-ee-air pref-air-ay)

My favorite subject is ...
Ma matière préférée est ...

(ma mat-ee-air pref-air-ay eh)

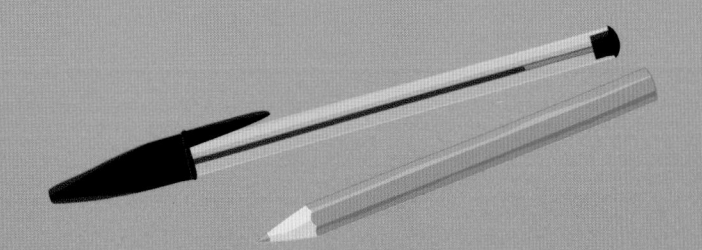

It's easy.
C'est facile.

(seh fa-seel)

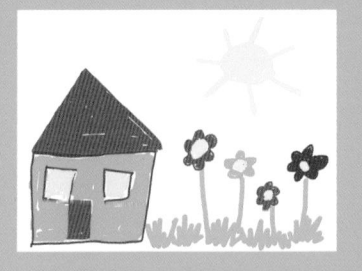

art
le dessin

(luh deh-sah)

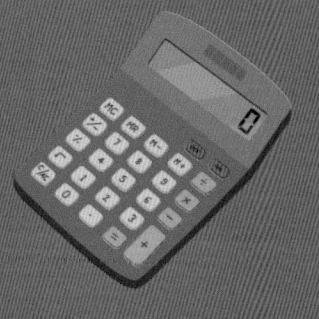

math
les maths

(lay mat)

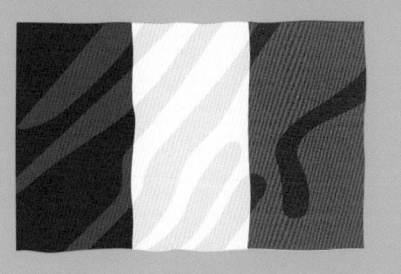

geography
la géographie

(la jhay-og-raf-ee)

French
le français

(luh fron-say)

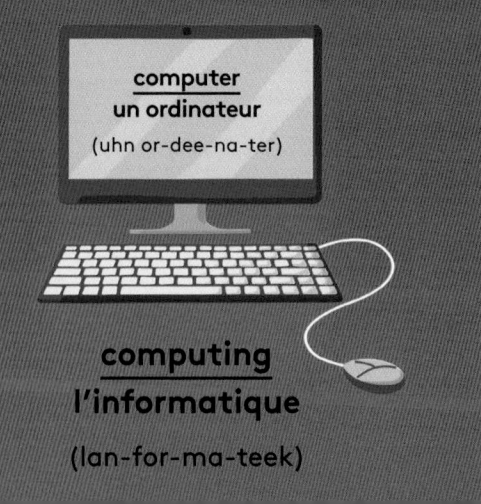

computer
un ordinateur

(uhn or-dee-na-ter)

computing
l'informatique

(lan-for-ma-teek)

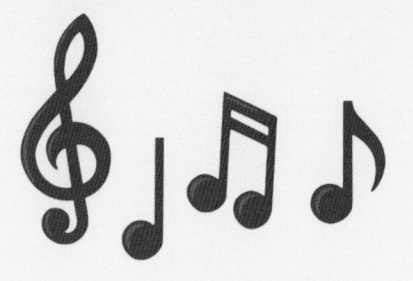

music
la musique

(la moo-zeek)

I don't like ...
Je n'aime pas ...
(jhuh nem pa)

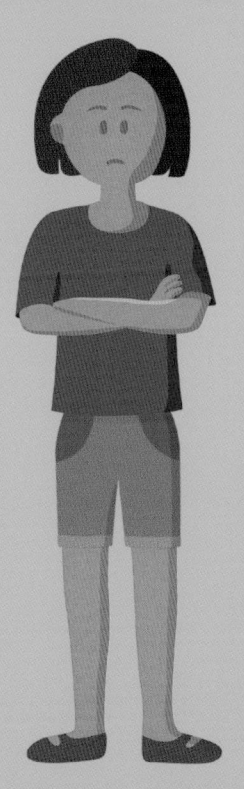

It's difficult.
C'est difficile.

(seh dif-ee-seel)

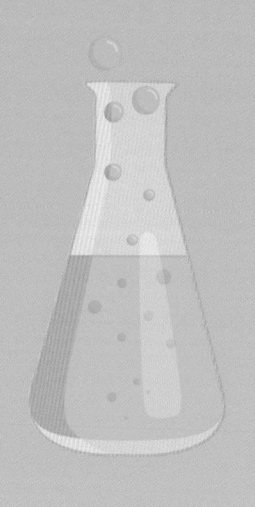

science
les sciences

(lay see-onss)

history
l'histoire

(lis-twar)

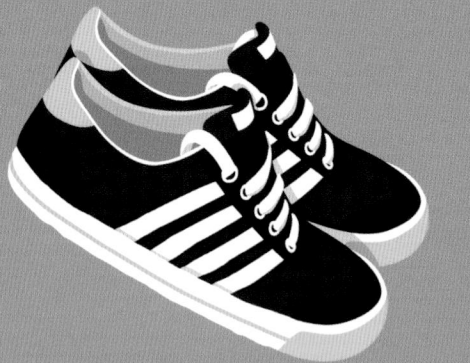

PE
l'ÉPS

(lay-pay-ess)

cooking
la cuisine

(la kwiz-een)

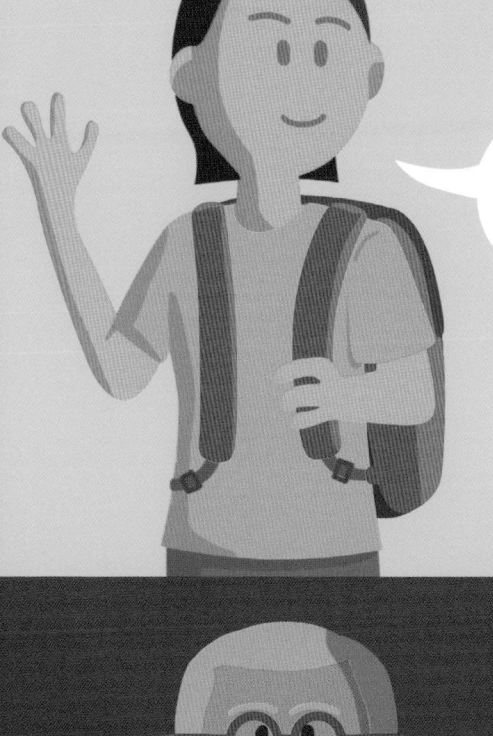

My teacher is great.
Mon professeur est génial.

(mon pro-fess-uhr eh jhen-ee-al)

My teacher is helpful.
Mon professeur est serviable.

(mon pro-fess-uhr eh sair-vee-a-bluh)

My teacher is strict!
Mon professeur est sévère!

(mon pro-fess-uhr eh sev-air)

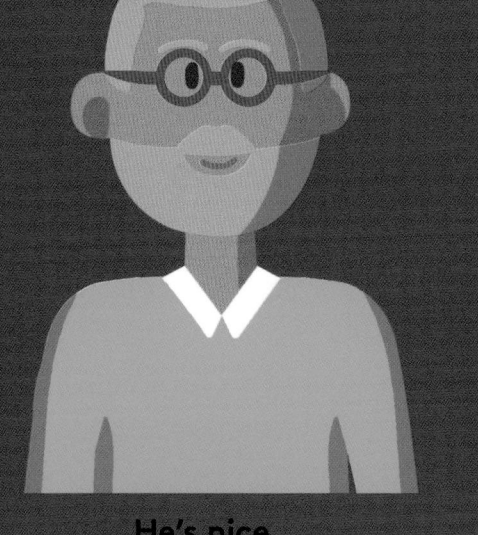

He's nice.
Il est gentil.

(eel eh jhon-tee)

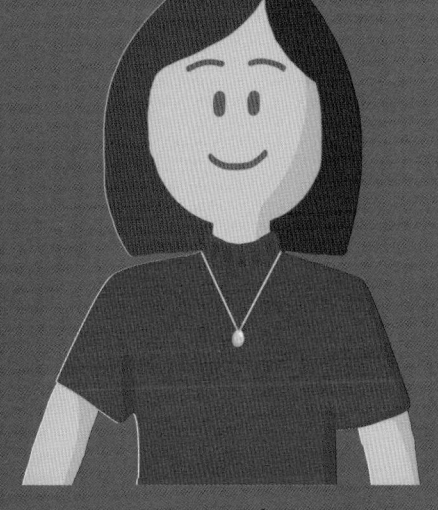

She's friendly.
Elle est amicale.

(el eh a-mee-kal)

What is your teacher called?
Comment s'appelle ton professeur?

(ko-mon sa-pel ton pro-fess-uhr)

My teacher is called …
Mon professeur s'appelle …

(mon pro-fess-uhr sa-pel)

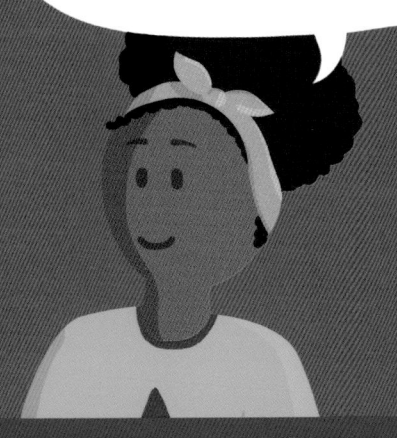

Can we sit together?
Asseyons-nous ensemble?

(a-say-on noo on-som-bluh)

Let's be friends!
Soyons amis!

(swa-yon am-ee)

Do you need help with your work?
As-tu besoin d'aide avec ton travail de classe?

(a-too buh-zwan d-ayd a-vek ton trav-eye duh class)

What's in your bag?
Qu'est-ce qu'il y a dans ton sac?
(kes keel ya don ton sak)

I have ...
J'ai ...
(jhay)

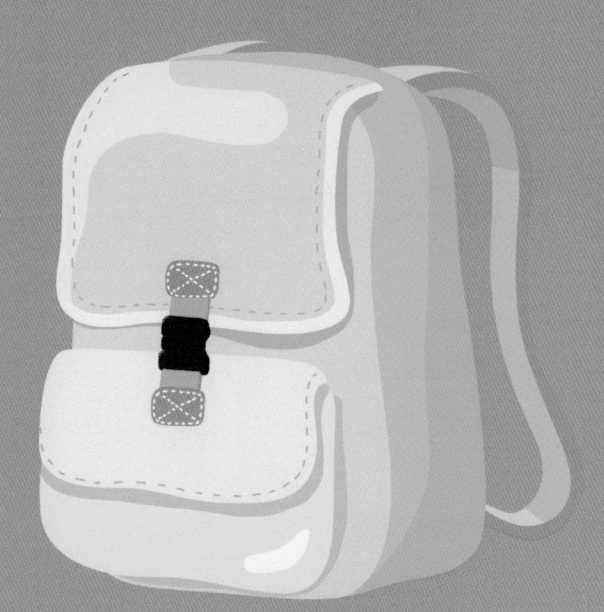

What's that?
Qu'est-ce que c'est?
(kes kuh seh)

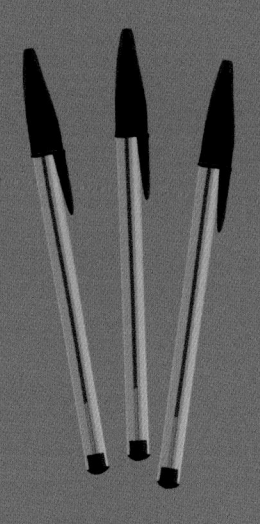

some pens
des stylos

(day stee-loh)

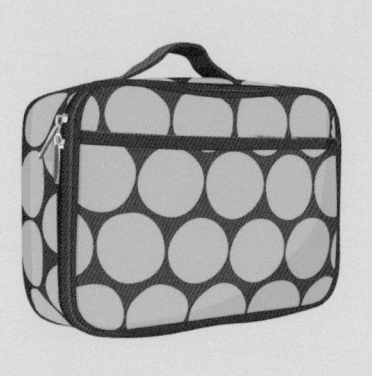

my lunch box
ma boîte à repas

(ma bwat a ruh-pa)

a bottle of water
une bouteille d'eau

(oon boo-tay doh)

a book
un livre

(uh leev-ruh)

131

Where is the pencil?
Où est le crayon?

(oo eh luh kray-on)

The pencil is …
Le crayon est …

(luh kray-on eh)

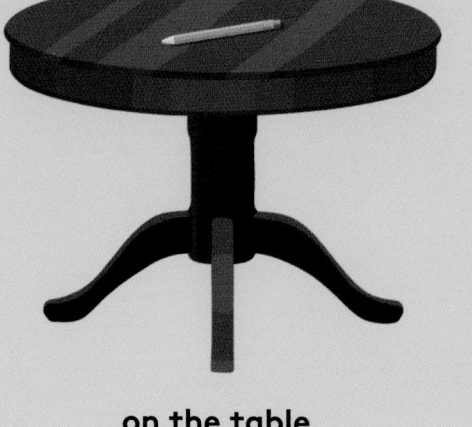

on the table
sur la table

(syur la ta-bluh)

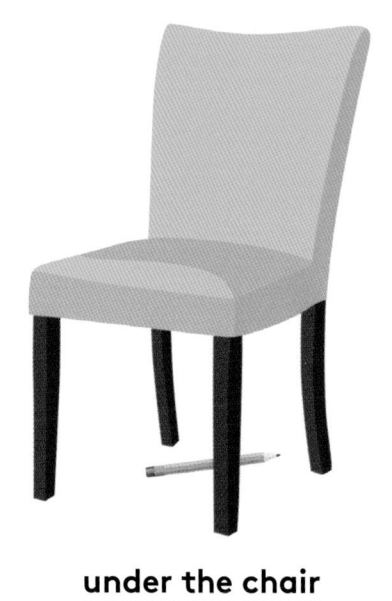

under the chair
sous la chaise

(soo la shez)

inside the pencil case
dans la trousse

(don la trooss)

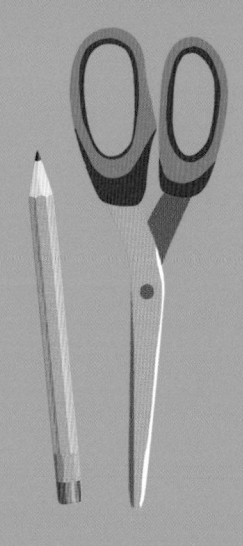

next to the scissors
à côté des ciseaux

(a koh-tay day see-zoh)

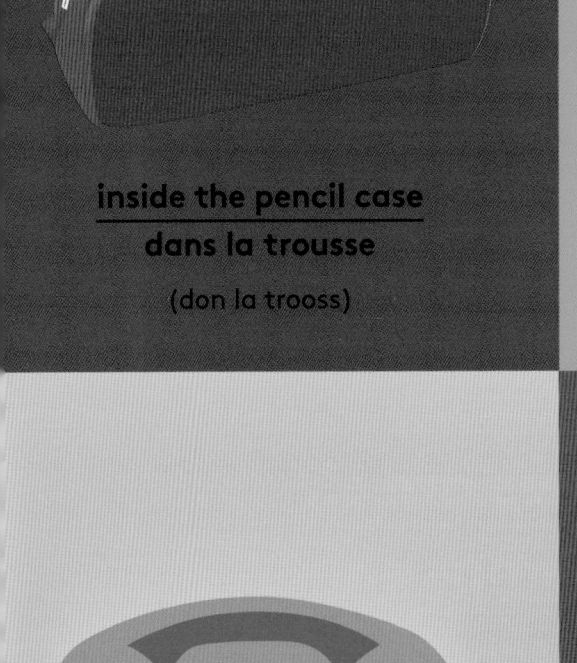

in front of the telephone
devant le téléphone

(duh-vont luh teh-leh-fon)

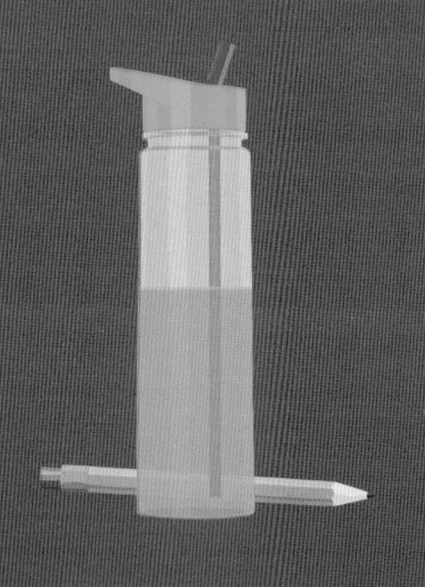

behind the bottle
derrière la bouteille

(deh-ree-air la boo-tay)

133

My hobby is ...
Mon passe-temps est ...
(mon pass-tahn eh)

My hobbies are ...
Mes passe-temps sont ...
(may pass-tahn sont)

What are your hobbies?
Quels sont tes passe-temps?

(kel sont tay pass-tahn)

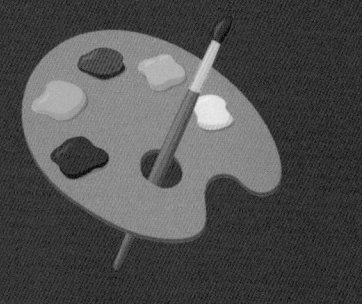

painting
la peinture

(la pan-tewr)

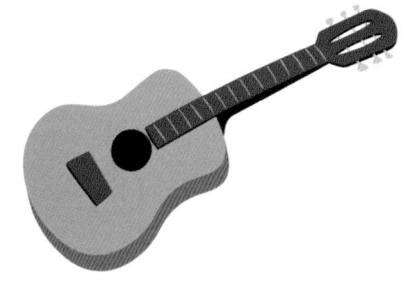

playing the guitar
jouer de la guitare

(jhoo-ay duh la gee-tar)

reading
la lecture

(la lek-tewr)

watching movies
regarder des films

(ruh-gar-day day feelm)

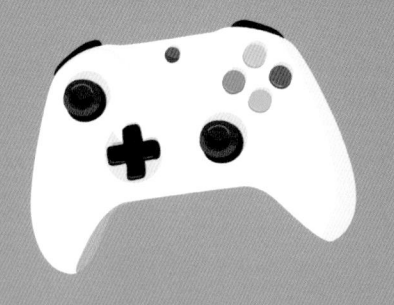

playing video games
jouer à des jeux vidéo

(jhoo-ay a day jhuh vid-ay-oh)

dancing
la danse

(la dahns)

135

What is your favorite sport?
Quel est ton sport préféré?
(kel eh ton spor pref-air-ay)

My favorite sport is ...
Mon sport préféré est ...
(mon spor pref-air-ay eh)

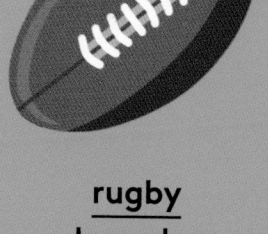

rugby
le rugby
(luh rug-bee)

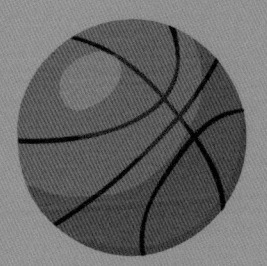

basketball
le basket-ball
(luh bask-et-bol)

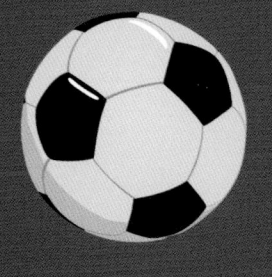

soccer
le football
(luh fewt-bol)

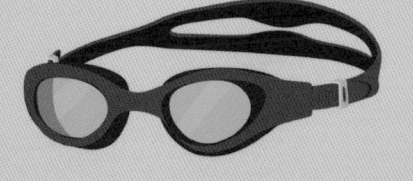

swimming
la natation
(la na-ta-see-on)

hockey
le hockey

(luh o-kee)

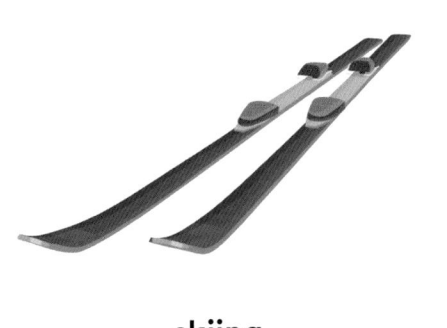

skiing
le ski

(luh skee)

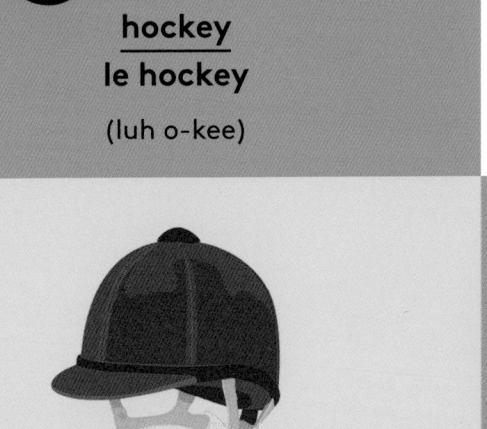

horseback riding
l'équitation

(lek-ee-tass-ee-yon)

volleyball
le volley-ball

(luh voh-lay-bol)

baseball
le base-ball

(luh bayz-bol)

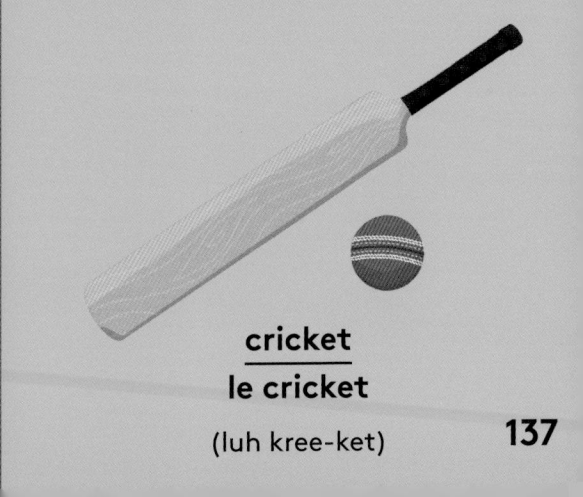

cricket
le cricket

(luh kree-ket)

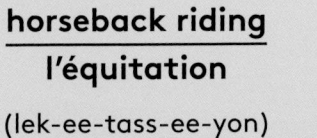

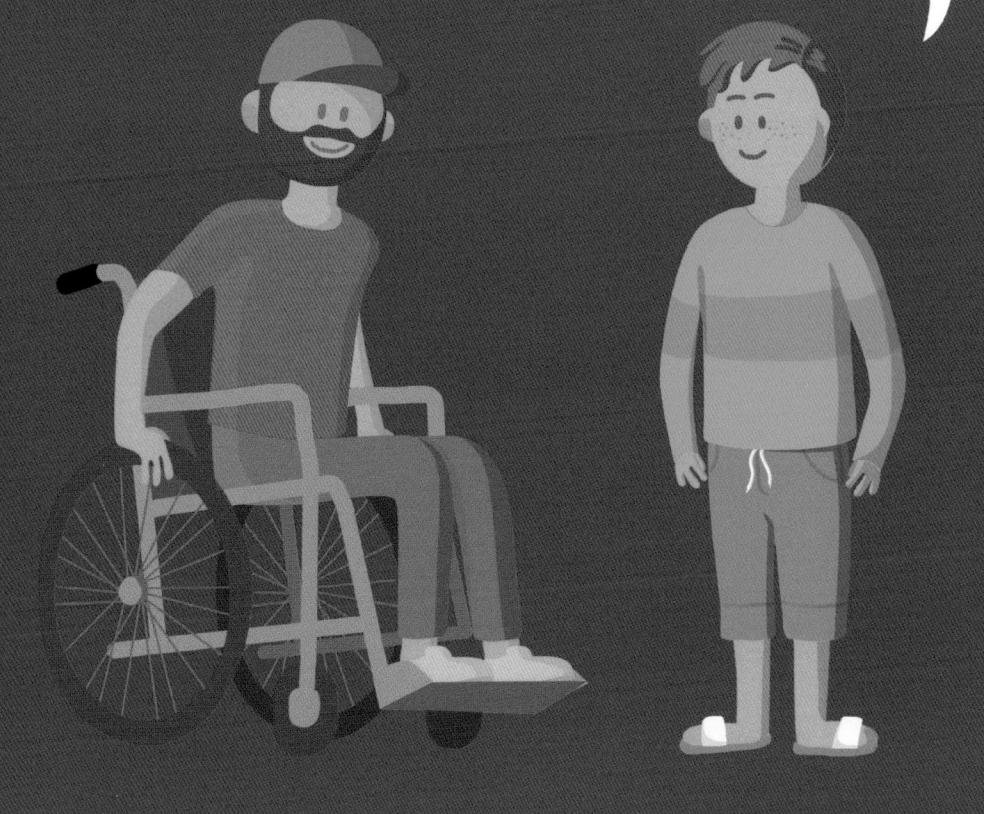

138

If you are female, you would say "je suis allée ... ." The pronunciation would remain the same.

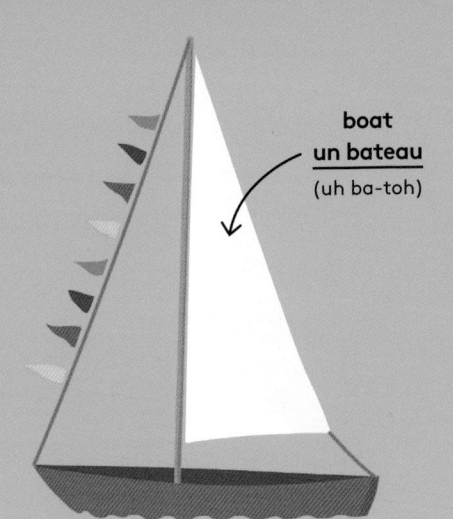

boat
un bateau
(uh ba-toh)

I went to a party
je suis allé à une fête

(jhuh swee a-lay a oon fet)

I went sailing
j'ai fait de la voile

(jhay fay duh la vwal)

I didn't do my homework!
Je n'ai pas fait mes devoirs!

(jhuh nay pa fay may duh-vwar)

I went bowling
j'ai fait du bowling

(jhay fay doo boh-ling)

I did my homework
j'ai fait mes devoirs

(jhay fay may duh-vwar)

139

What are you doing next weekend?
Qu'est-ce que tu vas faire le week-end prochain?
(kes kuh too va fair luh week-end pro-shan)

Next weekend I'm ...
Le week-end prochain je vais ...
(le week-end pro-shan jhuh vay)

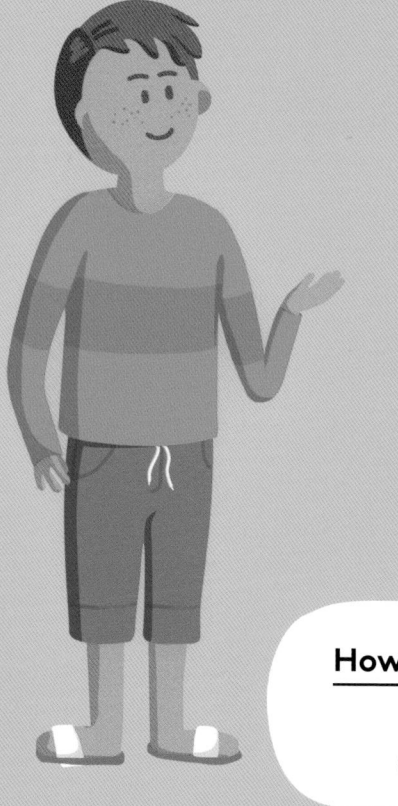

How about you?
Et toi?
(eh twah)

going ice skating
faire du patinage à glace
(fair doo pat-in-ar-jh a glas)

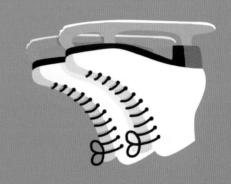

going to play tennis
jouer au tennis
(jhoo-ay oh ten-eess)

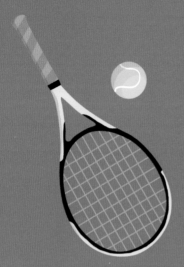

going cycling
faire du vélo
(fair doo vay-loh)

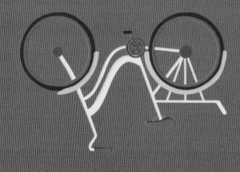

going to the beach
aller à la plage
(a-lay a la pla-jh)

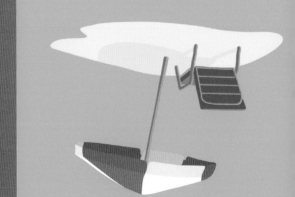

Let's bake a cake.
Allons faire un gâteau.
(al-on fair uh ga-toh)

We will need ...
Nous aurons besoin d'...
(nooz or-on buh-zwan d')

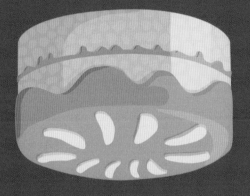

We need ingredients, too!
Nous avons aussi besoin des ingrédients!
(nooz av-on oh-see buh-zwan dayz an-gray-day-an)

an oven
un four
(uh fwor)

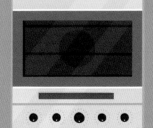

a recipe
une recette
(oon reh-set)

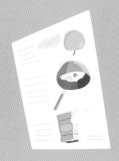

a whisk
un fouet
(uh fway)

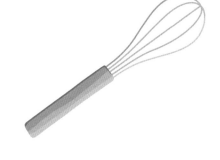

I'll help you wash the dishes.
Je t'aide à faire la vaisselle.
(jhuh tayd a fair la vay-sel)

scales
une balance
(oon ba-lons)

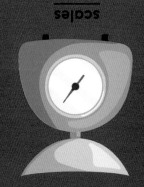

an apron
un tablier
(uh tab-lee-ay)

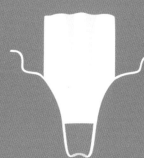

I saw …
J'ai vu …
(jhay voo)

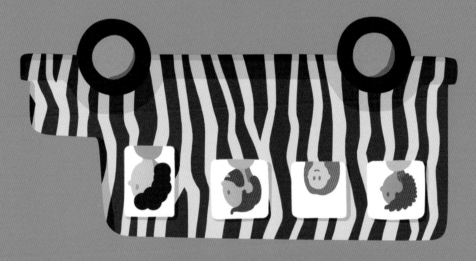

Yesterday I went to the zoo.
Hier je suis allé au zoo.
(ee-air jhuh sweez a-lay oh zoh)

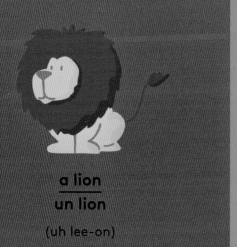

a lion
un lion

(uh lee-on)

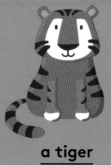

a tiger
un tigre

(uh tee-gruh)

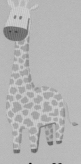

a giraffe
une girafe

(oon jhee-raf)

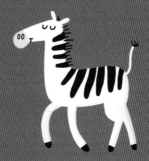

a zebra
un zèbre

(uh zair-bruh)

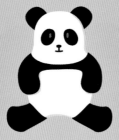

a panda
un panda

(uh pon-da)

I had a great time!
Je me suis très bien amusé!

(jhuh muh swee tray
bee-an a-moo-zay)

145

My favorite animal is ...
Mon animal préféré est ...
(mon an-ee-mal pref-air-ay eh)

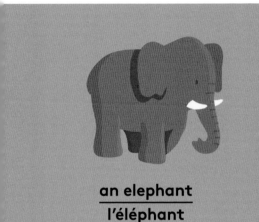

an elephant
l'éléphant

(leh-leh-fon)

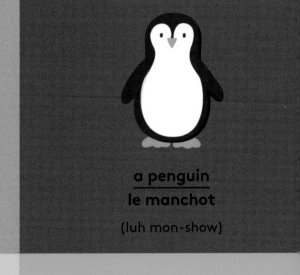

a penguin
le manchot

(luh mon-show)

an owl
le hibou

(luh ee-boo)

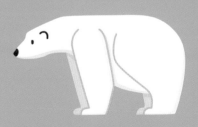

a polar bear
l'ours polaire

(lor poh-lair)

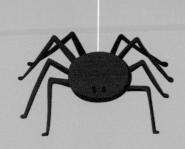

a spider
l'araignée

(la-ran-yay)

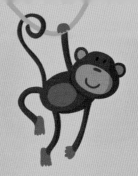

a monkey
le singe

(luh san-jh)

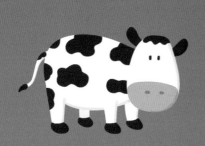

a cow
la vache

(la vash)

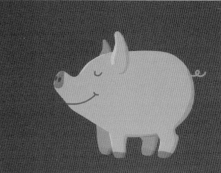

a pig
le cochon

(luh kosh-on)

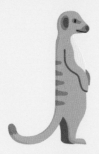

a meerkat
le suricate

(luh suh-ree-kat)

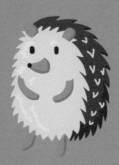

a hedgehog
le hérisson

(luh air-ees-on) **147**

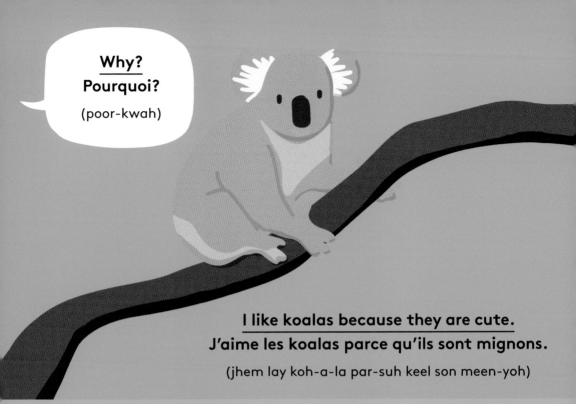

Why?
Pourquoi?
(poor-kwah)

I like koalas because they are cute.
J'aime les koalas parce qu'ils sont mignons.
(jhem lay koh-a-la par-suh keel son meen-yoh)

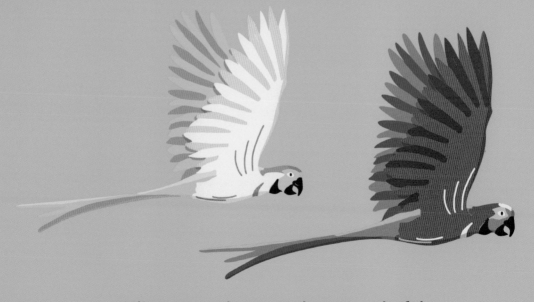

I like parrots because they are colorful.
J'aime les perroquets parce qu'ils sont colorés.
(jhem lay peh-roh-keh par-suh keel son kol-or-ay)

148

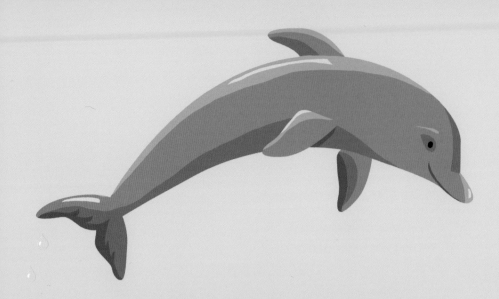

I like dolphins because they are clever.
J'aime les dauphins parce qu'ils sont intelligents.

(jhem lay doh-fan par-suh keel son an-tell-ee-jhon)

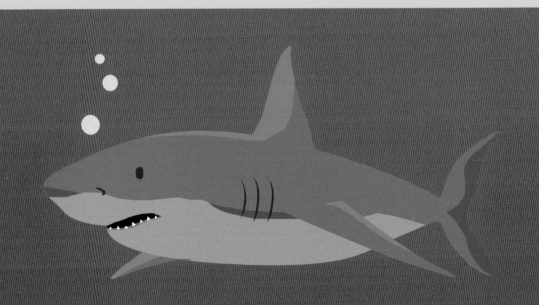

I like sharks because they are scary!
J'aime les requins parce qu'ils sont effrayants!

(jhem lay reh-kan par-suh keel son ef-ray-on)

In French, there is no need to say "a" when talking about professions.

I want to be ...
Je veux être ...
(jhuh vuh air-tr)

What do you want
to be when you grow up?
Que veux-tu faire quand tu seras grand(e)?
(kuh vuh-too fair kan too suh-ra gron[d])

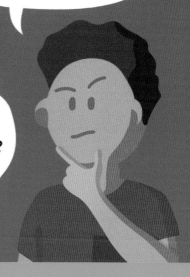

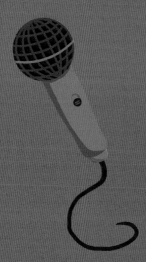

a singer
chanteur (m) / chanteuse (f)
(shon-tuhr / shon-tuhz)

a firefighter
pompier (m) / pompière (f)
(pom-pee-yay / pom-pee-air)

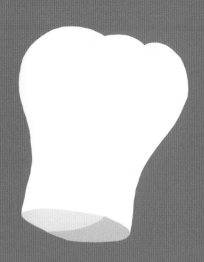

a chef
chef de cuisine

(shev duh kwiz-een)

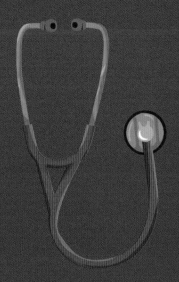

a doctor
médecin

(med-san)

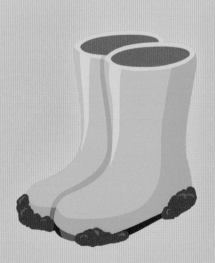

a farmer
fermier (m) / fermière (f)

(fair-mee-yay / fair-mee-air)

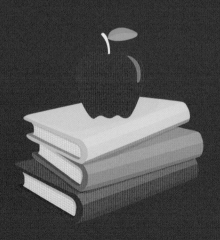

a teacher
professeur

(pro-fess-uhr)

151

What job would you like?
Quel métier aimerais-tu?

(kel met-yay em-uhr-ay-too)

I'm not sure.
Je ne suis pas sûr.

(jhuh nuh swee pa see-uhr)

Would you like to be ...
Aimerais-tu être ...

(em-uhr-ay-tu air-tr)

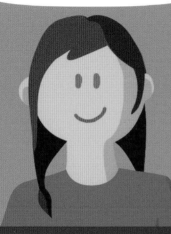

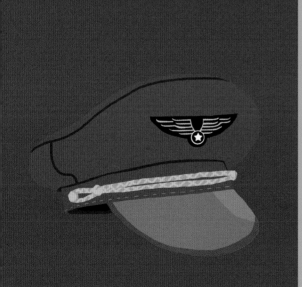

a pilot?
pilote?

(pee-lot)

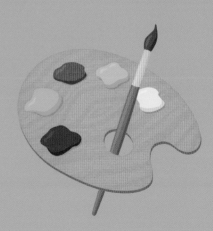

an artist?
artiste?

(ar-teest)

152

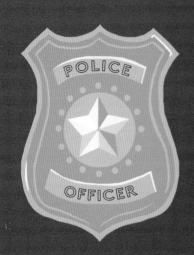

a police officer?
policier (m) / policière (f)?

(po-lees-ee-ay / po-lees-ee-air)

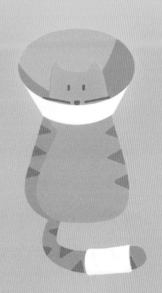

a vet?
vétérinaire?

(vet-eh-rin-air)

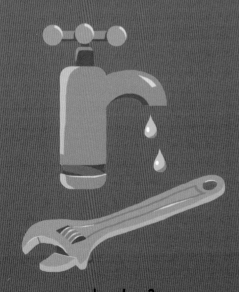

a plumber?
plombier (m) / plombière (f)?

(plom-bee-yay / plom-bee-air)

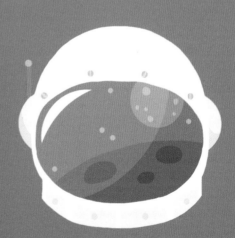

an astronaut?
astronaute?

(ast-roh-nort)

153

Are you going on vacation?
Vas-tu en vacances?

(va-too on va-konss)

I'm not going on vacation.
Je ne vais pas en vacances.

(jhuh nuh vay pa on va-konss)

I'm staying at home.
Je reste à la maison.

(jhuh rest a la may-zon)

Yes, I'm going ...
Oui, je vais ...

(wee jhuh vay)

to Mexico
au Mexique

(oh meks-eek)

to the Netherlands
aux Pays-Bas

(oh pay-ba)

to Canada
au Canada

(oh ka-na-da)

to China
en Chine

(on sheen)

to Germany
en Allemagne

(on al-uh-man-yuh)

to Turkey
en Turquie

(on tuhr-kee)

154

to Spain
en Espagne

(on es-pan-yuh)

to the United States
aux États-Unis

(ohz ay-tat-oo-nee)

to Australia
en Australie

(on ost-ra-lee)

to Greece
en Grèce

(on gress)

to France
en France

(on fronss)

to the
United Kingdom
au Royaume-Uni

(oh rwa-yom-oon-ee)

to Thailand
en Thaïlande

(on tye-lond)

to Italy
en Italie

(on ee-tal-ee)

to South Africa
en Afrique du Sud

(on a-freek doo sood)

to Japan
au Japon

(oh jha-pon)

to New Zealand
en Nouvelle-Zélande

(on noo-vel-zay-lond)

to Switzerland
en Suisse

(on sweess)

Where are you staying?
Où restes-tu?
(oo rest-too)

I'm staying in ...
Je reste dans ...
(jhuh rest donz)

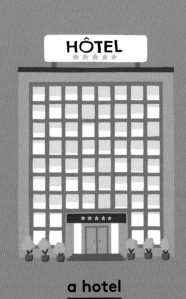

a hotel
un hôtel
(uhn oh-tel)

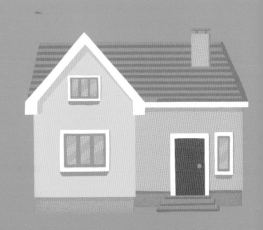

a house
une maison
(oon may-zon)

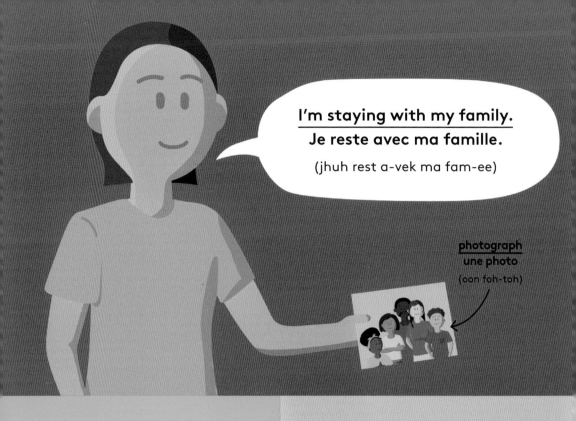

I'm staying with my family.
Je reste avec ma famille.
(jhuh rest a-vek ma fam-ee)

photograph
une photo
(oon foh-toh)

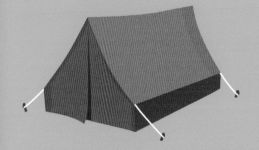

a tent
une tente
(oon tont)

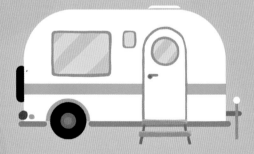

a trailer
une caravane
(oon ka-ra-van)

157

How are you getting there?
Comment vas-tu y aller?
(ko-mon va-too ee a-lay)

I'm going by ...
Je vais aller ...
(jhuh vay a-lay)

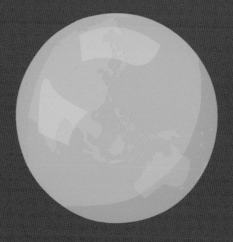

Traveling is fun!
Les voyages sont amusants!
(lay vwa-yar-jh sont am-oo-zont)

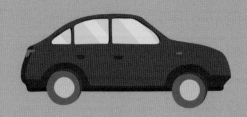

car
en voiture

(on vwa-tewr)

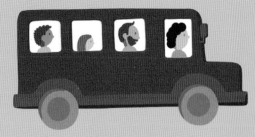

bus
en autobus

(on o-toh-boos)

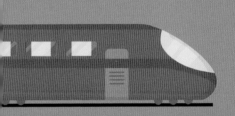

train
en train

(on tra)

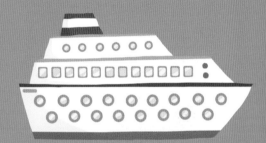

ferry
en ferry

(on fair-ay)

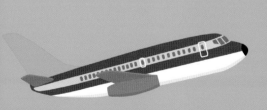

airplane
en avion

(on av-ee-on)

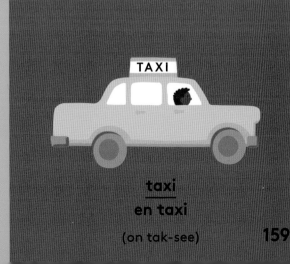

taxi
en taxi

(on tak-see)

> **What are you taking?**
> **Que prends-tu?**
> (kuh prond-too)

I'm taking ...
Je prends ...
(jhuh prond)

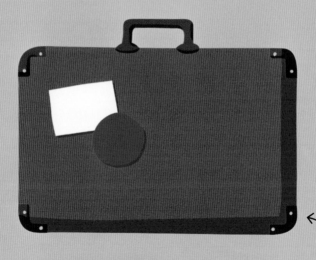

suitcase
la valise
(la va-leez)

160

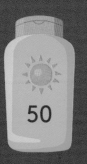

my sunscreen
ma crème solaire

(ma krem soh-lair)

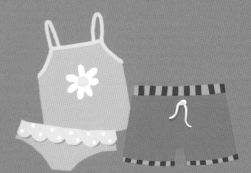

a swimsuit
un maillot de bain

(uh mye-oh duh ban)

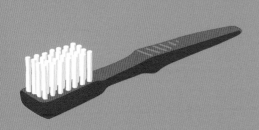

my toothbrush
ma brosse à dents

(ma bross a don)

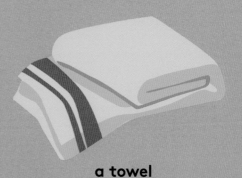

a towel
une serviette

(oon sair-vee-et)

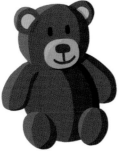

my teddy bear
mon nounours

(mon noo-noorz)

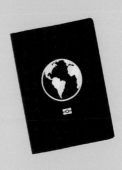

my passport
mon passeport

(mon pass-por)

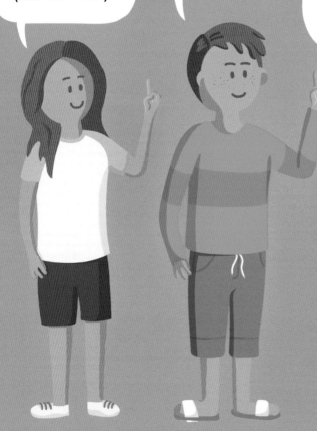
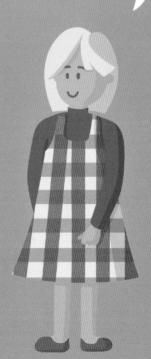

How long are you staying?
Tu vas passer combien de temps?

(too va pa-say kom-bee-an duh tahn)

Two weeks.
Deux semaines.

(duh suh-men)

One week.
Une semaine.

(oon suh-men)

Just a few days.
Seulement quelques jours.

(suhl-mon kel-kuh jhor)

It will be amazing!
Ça sera sensationnel!

(sa suh-ra son-sass-ee-on-el)

It sounds lovely.
Cela me semble bien.

(seh-la muh som-bluh bee-yen)

Have a good trip!
Bon voyage!

(bon voy-ar-jh)

See you in a little while.
À plus tard.

(a ploo tar)

Enjoy!
Amuse-toi bien!

(a-mooz-twa bee-an)

Goodbye.
Au revoir.

(oh r-vwar)

Vocabulary list

Here is a list of English words, along with their French translations. All of these words can be found within the phrases featured in this book.

Some nouns and adjectives change in the feminine form. To make these words feminine, add the letters shown after the word in parentheses. If the feminine word is very different, the full spelling is given.

a /an	un(e)	bowling (*noun*)	le bowling
afternoon	l'après-midi [*masc.*]	boy	un garçon
airplane	un avion	bread	le pain
ambulance	une ambulance	breakfast	le petit déjeuner
and	et	brother	un frère
angry	faché(e)	brown	brun(e)
animal	un animal	bucket	un seau
apple	une pomme	burger	un hamburger
apron	un tablier	bus	un autobus
art	le dessin	but	mais
artist	un(e) artiste	butcher (*shop*)	une boucherie
astronaut	un(e) astronaute	butter	le beurre
aunt	une tante		
		café	un café
bad	mauvais(e)	cake	un gâteau
bag	un sac	candy (*noun*)	un bonbon
bakery	une boulangerie	cap (*hat*)	une casquette
balloon	un ballon	car	une voiture
banana	une banane	card	une carte
bank	une banque	cardigan	un cardigan
baseball	le base-ball	carrot	une carotte
basket	un panier	cash register	une caisse
basketball	le basket-ball	cat	un chat
beach	une plage	cell phone	un portable
beard	une barbe	chair	une chaise
because	parce que	check (*noun*)	une addition
bed	un lit	cheese	le fromage
behind	derrière	chef	un(e) chef de cuisine
bike	un vélo	chicken	le poulet
bird	un oiseau	chocolate	le chocolat
birthday	un anniversaire	choice	un choix
black	noir(e)	city	une grande ville
blond	blond(e)	clever	intelligent(e)
blue	bleu(e)	clock	une horloge
boat	un bateau	closed (*adj*)	fermé(e)
book (*noun*)	un livre	cloud	un nuage
boot	une botte	coat	un manteau
bottle	une bouteille	coconut	une noix de coco
bowl (*noun*)	un bol	coffee	un café

cola	un coca	fire (*noun*)	un feu
cold (*adj*)	froid(e)	firefighter	un(e) pompier (pompière)
cold (*noun*)	un rhume	first aid	les premiers secours [*masc.*]
color	une couleur	fish (*noun*)	un poisson
computer	un ordinateur	flower	une fleur
computing	l'informatique [*fem.*]	fog	le brouillard
cooking	la cuisine	fork	une fourchette
cough (*noun*)	une toux	freckles	les taches de rousseur [*fem.*]
countryside	la campagne	friend	un(e) ami(e)
cousin	un(e) cousin(e)	friendly	amical(e)
cow	une vache	fries	les frites [*fem.*]
crazy	fou (folle)	fruit	les fruits [*masc.*]
credit card	une carte de crédit	fun (*adj*)	amusant(e)
cricket (*sport*)	le cricket	funny	drôle
crossroads	un carrefour		
curly	bouclé(e)	game	un jeu
cute	mignon(ne)	geography	la géographie
		giraffe	une girafe
delicious	délicieux (délicieuse)	girl	une fille
difficult	difficile	glass (*vessel*)	un verre
dinner	le dîner	glasses	les lunettes [*fem.*]
dirty	sale	glove	un gant
doctor	un médecin	good	bien/bon(ne)
dog	un chien	goodbye	au revoir
dolphin	un dauphin	grandfather	un grandpère
dress (*noun*)	une robe	grandmother	une grandmère
drink (*noun*)	une boisson	gray	gris(e)
dry	sec (sèche)	green	vert(e)
		guitar	une guitare
easy	facile		
egg	un œuf	hair	les cheveux [*masc.*]
elephant	un éléphant	hairbrush	une brosse à cheveux
emergency	une urgence	ham	le jambon
evening	le soir	hamster	un hamster
excited	impatient(e)	happy	heureux (heureuse)
expensive	cher (chère)	hat (*winter*)	un bonnet
eye	un œil [*plural - des yeux*]	hazelnut	une noisette
		hedgehog	un hérisson
fall	l'automne [*masc.*]	hello	bonjour
family	une famille	helpful	serviable
farmer	un(e) fermier (fermière)	hi	salut
father	un père	history	l'histoire [*fem.*]
favorite	préféré(e)	hobby	un passe-temps
ferry	un ferry	hockey	le hockey
fever	une fièvre	home	une maison
fine (*adv*)	bien	homework	les devoirs [*masc.*]

horse	un cheval	minute	une minute
horseback riding	l'équitation [*fem.*]	money	l'argent [*masc.*]
hospital	un hôpital	monkey	un singe
hot	chaud(e)	moon	la lune
hotel	un hôtel	more	plus
house	une maison	more than	plus que
how	comment	morning	le matin
hungry	faim	mother	une mère
		mouse	une souris
I	je/j'	movie (*noun*)	un film
ice cream	une glace	movie theater	un cinéma
ice skating (*noun*)	le patinage à glace	mug	une tasse
idea	une idée	music	la musique
in front of	devant	mustache	une moustache
ingredient	un ingrédient		
		name	un nom
juice	un jus	napkin	une serviette
		necklace	un collier
ketchup	le ketchup	nervous	nerveux (nerveuse)
key	une clé	night	la nuit
key ring	un porte-clés	no	non
kite	un cerf-volant	noisy	bruyant(e)
knife	un couteau	noodles	les nouilles [*fem.*]
koala	un koala	notepad	un cahier
		nothing	rien
language	une langue	nut	une noix
left (*not right*)	gauche		
lemonade	une limonade	old	vieux/vieil (vieille)
lion	un lion	on	sur
lizard	un lézard	open (*adj*)	ouvert(e)
long	long(ue)	or	ou
lunch	le déjeuner	orange (*adj*)	orange
lunch box	une boîte à repas	orange (*fruit*)	une orange
		oven	un four
map	une carte	over there	là-bas
market	un marché	owl	un hibou
math	les maths [*fem.*]		
maybe	peut-être	panda	un panda
me	moi	pants	un pantalon
medicine	le médicament	parent	un parent
meerkat	un suricate	park (*noun*)	un parc
menu	une carte	parrot	un perroquet
midday	midi [*masc.*]	party (*noun*)	une fête
midnight	minuit [*masc.*]	passport	un passeport
milk	le lait	pasta	les pâtes [*fem.*]
mint	la menthe	PE	l'ÉPS [*fem.*]

pen	un stylo	science	les sciences [*fem.*]
pencil	un crayon	scissors	les ciseaux [*masc.*]
pencil case	une trousse	season (*time*)	la saison
penguin	un manchot	shampoo	le shampooing
pepper (*spice*)	le poivre	shark	un requin
pharmacy	une pharmacie	shellfish	les fruits de mer [*masc.*]
phone	un téléphone	shirt	une chemise
photograph	une photo	shoe	une chaussure
pig	un cochon	shopping cart	un chariot
pilot	un(e) pilote	shopping list	une liste des courses
pineapple	un ananas	short	court(e)
pink	rose	shorts	un short
pistachio	une pistache	shovel	une pelle
pizza	une pizza	since	depuis
plate	une assiette	singer	un(e) chanteur (chanteuse)
playful	enjoué(e)	sister	une sœur
please	s'il vous plaît	skiing (*noun*)	le ski
plumber	un(e) plombier (plombière)	slice (*noun*)	une tranche
poison	le poison	small	petit(e)
polar bear	un ours polaire	soap	le savon
police	la police	soccer	le football
police officer	un(e) policier (policière)	sock	une chaussette
postcard	une carte postale	some	quelques
post office	un bureau de poste	sorry	pardon
present	un cadeau	spider	une araignée
purple	violet(te)	spoon	une cuillère
		sport	un sport
rabbit	un lapin	spot	une tache
rain	la pluie	spring (*season*)	le printemps
rainbow	un arc-en-ciel	stamp (*noun*)	un timbre
ready	prêt(e)	star	l'étoile [*fem.*]
recipe	une recette	statue	une statue
red	rouge	stepbrother	un demi-frère
restaurant	un restaurant	storm (*noun*)	un orage
restroom	les toilettes [*fem.*]	straight	droit(e)
right (*not left*)	droit(e)	straight (*hair*)	raide
rugby	le rugby	strawberry	une fraise
		strict	sévère
sad	triste	stripe	une rayure
salad	une salade verte	subject (*school*)	la matière
sales assistant	un(e) vendeur (vendeuse)	suitcase	une valise
salt	le sel	summer	l'été [*masc.*]
sandwich	un sandwich	sun	le soleil
scarf	une écharpe	sunglasses	les lunettes de soleil [*fem.*]
scary	effrayant(e)	sunscreen	la crème solaire
school	l'école [*fem.*]	supermarket	un supermarché

sweater	un pull	vacations	les vacances [fem.]
swimming (noun)	la natation	vanilla	la vanille
swimming pool	une piscine	very	très
swimsuit	un maillot de bain	vet	un(e) vétérinaire
		video game	un jeu vidéo
table	une table	village	un village
tall	grand(e)	volleyball	le volley-ball
taxi	un taxi		
teacher	un(e) professeur	wallet	un porte-monnaie
teddy bear	un nounours	washcloth	un gant de toilette
tennis	le tennis	watch (noun)	une montre
tent	une tente	water (noun)	l'eau [fem.]
thank you	merci	we	nous
the	le (la)/l'/les	weather	le temps
their	leur	week	une semaine
they	ils (elles)	weekend	un week-end
thirsty	soif	weighing scales	une balance
ticket	un billet	welcome	bienvenue
tie (noun)	une cravate	well (adv)	bien
tiger	un tigre	wet	mouillé(e)
time (noun)	l'heure [fem.]	wheat	le blé
tired	fatigué(e)	when	quand
today	aujourd'hui	where	où
together	ensemble	whisk (noun)	un fouet
toilet paper	le papier hygiénique	white	blanc(he)
tomato	une tomate	who	qui
tomorrow	demain	why	pourquoi
toothbrush	une brosse à dents	Wi-Fi	le WiFi
toothpaste	le dentifrice	wind (weather)	le vent
torn	déchiré(e)	winter	l'hiver [masc.]
towel	une serviette	with	avec
town	une ville	without	sans
toy (noun)	un jouet	wonderful	merveilleux (merveilleuse)
traffic circle	un rond-point		
traffic lights	les feux [masc.]	yellow	jaune
trailer	une caravane	yes	oui
train (noun)	un train	yesterday	hier
train station	une gare	young	jeune
tree	un arbre	yo-yo	un yoyo
trip (noun)	un voyage		
T-shirt	un tee-shirt	zebra	un zèbre
		zoo	un zoo
umbrella	un parapluie		
uncle	un oncle		
under	sous		